Elites, Technology, and Asset Prices

–

The politics of technological shifts

Imprint:

Andreas Antrup, Berlin, Germany

ISBN: 978-3-00-080212-6

Independently published

Prologue

This book explores a simple thesis: Not only does technology govern how much wealth societies can generate but also how it gets distributed between elites and commoners - and it determines what social structures prevail. Most of human recorded history is about agrarian societies with a hereditary elite and commoners squeezed to just so survive. Manufacturing brought genuine democracy, mass education and shared prosperity. Computers and artificial intelligence will push commoners into low level service jobs and bring societies back closer to agrarian times.

It turns out that perpetual increases in living standards are not a God-given right, our hunter-gatherer-turned-peasant forebears could attest to that. And in fact, human rights and democracy are not sacrosanct either and will be retired. Or perhaps rather decay into theatrics much like European monarchies did in the 20th century. We will live either in futuristic merchant republics or in neo-autocratic regimes. The anonymity of the big city will turn out to be a historical anomaly. And people's religious beliefs will change again, away from materialistic self-determination to a greater role of mysticism and "AI gurus". Assets and their prices may come to resemble the art market more than the erstwhile American frontier. And the big open questions are whether elites are going to be more benign and benevolent than in the past, under the guidance of their "AI consiglieri", and whether they will retain control or lose it to the machines.

The chapters are self-contained and so, dear reader, you may jump back and forth. Before jumping head-in, chapters 1 and 2 outline why and how elites are drawn to hinder technological change and what forces them to embrace it, along with new elite members and all the ensuing dilution of power. Chapters 3 through 5 review how past and future technological shifts, from hunter gatherer times to agriculture, from agriculture to manufacturing, and from manufacturing to information technology and artificial intelligence impact elite and commoner relationships as well as the societal setup and structure. Chapters 6 to 8 explore in deep dives the implications on data, privacy and organisational as well as societal decision-making, the implications on what is truth, what is the moral compass, and what is religion, the implications on asset creation and asset prices. The final chapter attempts a "so what" of what we will have learnt by the time we reach the end of the book. An afterword on common myths and misconceptions concludes.

It is said that predictions are a risky business, especially if they concern the future. Same with policy recommendations. And yet, predictions and policy recommendations are the icing on the cake of the commentary of political economy. Take this short book as a remedy to our overly soft, overly cautious cuisine: Of the words that follow, 61% concern the future.

Chapter 1: Pride, prejudice, fear, and technology

"...and the report which was in general circulation within five minutes after his entrance, of his having ten thousand a year."
Jane Austen, 1813

Imagine you are one of the Darcys, Fitzwilliam or Elisabeth, just after their marriage at the conclusion of Jane Austen's novel. Your home at Pemberley in the English countryside is as idyllic as ever, and with 10'000 pounds to yourselves a year there is scarcely a constraint on your material desires. It may well be early 1812, with England on its way to world domination and the future of your children assured. Or so it may seem to us now, looking back from the third millennium.

Back then in the spring of 1812, things looked a little different. Britain had been enduring the harsh effects of the Continental Blockade for five long years, and had been fighting Napoleon in a succession of wars for even longer. No wonder the idyllic countryside of the novel is full of men in uniform, including the devious Mr Wickham of the militia. With the victory at Trafalgar six years prior there was perhaps no imminent threat of invasion, but Napoleon was at the height of his power and only months away from invading Russia with the Grande Armée.

And into this fraught situation enter the Luddites. Over the past twelve months a wave of uprisings has called the English nobility, including you, off guard as angry mobs storm the newish factories and break the machines that sustain textile production. You have just got the news that the factory of your friend Frank Vickerman in West Yorkshire has also been attacked.

Revolts are a dangerous thing: today it is the factories, tomorrow it may well be Pemberley. And so, as you discuss the situation with the Bingleys and other friends of yours in high circles, what is your thinking?

Should the crown send in the military to suppress the workers revolt, stand guard outside of the factories and protect the wealth of the industrialists? Or should it dismantle the factories and give the mob their old jobs back, weaving cloths like it had been done, in peace, for centuries?

You remember that England had been through rebellion before: king Charles I was beheaded about a hundred and sixty years prior, having lost the Civil War to Oliver Cromwell. Why risk having a revolt spiral out of control again and losing your and your children's comfortable life? And all that risk just to save some upstart industrialists' concerns...

You wouldn't know at the time that protecting the factories would lead to the Industrial Revolution taking off. You wouldn't know at the time that this would enable the rise of the Empire. You wouldn't know at the time that this would lead to universal suffrage and the welfare state in the next century.

What you would know at the time is that Britain's situation was verging on the desperate: cut off from Europe except for some smuggling, and facing an emperor who could raise armies of hundreds of thousands and lead them with unmatched genius. Survival depended on the Royal Navy and trade with the colonies. And much of that trade in turn depended on the steady and increasing flow of textiles from the new factories.

In such a situation, what do you do? You take the bull by the horns. You send in an army of 12'000 men, crush the Luddites, and have their leaders hanged.

And that's indeed what transpired.

England is an odd place for the Industrial Revolution to have happened. Prior to the weaving machines and the steam engine, arguably no major invention was invented there. The printing press, double bookkeeping, the stock market, the compass, gunpowder – none of these things. They were invented where intuitively one would expect inventions to happen: in places where large populations build large and complex economies with both the demand for new solutions and the supply of educated brains and risk capital.

Scholars refer to things like the abundance of coal, the Enlightenment scientific revolution, the scarcity of labour, the English patent law system. But this misses a crucial factor: Technological progress was encouraged and protected by the elite, by people like you Darcys.

Perhaps without the shock of the Spanish Armada in 1588, and the ensuing triumph, England would not have developed into a naval power, and would not have sought value and riches from endeavours abroad, be it trade or colonies. But with that came an outwards orientation of the elite. Value is not only redistributed within the country, but taken from elsewhere. Take this outward orientation and then add in the threat from the much more populous continental European powers, a mere 34 km of waterway away – and what you get is an elite willing to accommodate upstart inventors, tinkerers and industrialists because the new industries they enable help to stave off these external threats.

Consider that the possibly most famous square in London is called Trafalgar Square. And that the largest railway station is called Waterloo Station. Two hundred years have passed, and the names of that existential struggle still stick.

We of course cannot be sure at this point of time what our investments and enablement of information technologies and artificial intelligence ("AI") will lead to fifty or a hundred years from now. But we can try to be smarter and farther looking out than the Darcys. But before we do, it is helpful to build an understanding of how political structures enable or suppress technological transitions or shifts, and how they change in response of these transitions.

Chapter 2: How transitions work

"A föld ne mozogjon, hanem álljon. – S ha az egész föld előremegy is, ez a darab föld, ami a mienk, ne menjen vele."
"The world shall not move, but stand still. – And if the whole world moved forward, this piece of land, which is ours, shall not move with it."
Kazimir Baradlay, country commissioner and large-scale landowner, a character of Mór Jókai's, 1869

Kazimir may have been an imaginative extreme case, but the sentiment that he espouses echoes throughout history:

(1) Elites are conservative

Elites have made it. By definition. And if you are at the top of the pyramid, the only way is down. So every change, everything that would rock the boat – is a threat.

This makes established elites inherently conservative. Their primary mindset is value preservation, not value creation. This makes good sense for them and they will deviate from this only if they feel forced to.

Technological change also rocks the boat. New technology is risky for the elite: it creates new sources of wealth and power. The inventors, the entrepreneurs driving new technologies and their adoption endanger the relative power of the incumbent elite simply by their success. Think of the industry magnates, the Rockefellers, the Krupps and others who rose to prominence and power on the back of their new technologies.

New technology also destroys established sources of wealth and power. As when gunpowder made horse-mounted knights and their castles vulnerable, and eventually obsolete. Or when aeroplanes made steam cruiser crossings of the Atlantic disappear. Or or or... The Schumpeterian creative destruction that is technological change (and with it economic growth) – is deeply disturbing to incumbent elites. New technology can also be difficult to control and it can have unintended consequences. The worst outcome from an elite perspective is to 'reset the game to start' by ushering in an enemy conquest or a revolution.

No wonder that throughout much of history elites have resisted change in their lands, perhaps most successfully in the Edo shogunate of Japan. For two and half centuries, technology, in particular warmaking technology was frozen and the country cut off from the outside world. This very successfully preserved the elite of the feudal agrarian society centred on the Samurai.

Apart from throttling technological change, there are other coping mechanisms for the incumbent elite. Needless to say over the long run societies that adopted coping mechanisms that enabled technological change have outcompeted the ones that simply stalled technology.

The two major enabling coping mechanism are co-opting new elite members and acquiring outsized stakes in new ventures.

Co-opting enables the incumbent elite to set the rules of the game of how to enter the elite and thus ensure a relatively favourable outcome for itself; this is evolution rather than revolution after all.

As an aside, we see co-opting also happening with 'local elites' after a conquest: as in the British Raj in the Indian subcontinent integrating existing Indian rulers into their colonial power structures as a tier two elite or 'quasi-elite', and thus outsourcing parts of the affairs of state them. This is a time-tested approach we also know from empires as diverse as the Roman Empire and the Mongol Empire. As an aside to the aside, local elites that were perceived to be technologically very retarded and thus of low value as outsourced administrators were typically done away with by the conquerors; see the native American elites in both North and South America who lost everything, or the rulers of many pre-colonial African kingdoms.

Securing an outsized stake in new ventures is a more novel approach. Perhaps one could also say that whereas co-opting is the 'feudal answer', stake acquisition is the 'bureaucratic answer'. In short, this second answer means securing a large share for the incumbent elite of the new value streams and wealth that are being generated by new technology.

This can happen through income and wealth taxes as done during pre-revolutionary France for instance: new technologies put to work to generate value and profit by traders and early industrialists were taxed and asked to buy government debt while the aristocrats buzzing around the king in Versailles were privileged to be taxation exempt.

Something similar happens in new guises in the contemporary developed world through the financial system. To illustrate, consider venture capital funds. Promising startups that bring disruptive new technologies to market and may generate large new riches are financed largely through investments by these funds. The trick is to fund many similar contenders (across the venture capital industry, not necessarily only one fund), which means that all contenders have to take on a lot of capital to burn through in their growth spurt. And the more capital you take in early on in the new venture's life, the more the stakes of the founders are handed over to funds or 'get diluted'. And they get diluted in favour of the capital providers which are, of course, the incumbent elite. This is how the modern-day elite secures its stake in the value creation of new technologies.

These coping mechanisms are all well and good, but if the incumbent elite can help it, they would rather not have much technological change. Owning and controlling the existing assets that generate value and preserving these through shielding them from competition is a much safer way to live the good life.

(2) A murder is committed

Murderers in detective stories are said to require two things to commit a murder: motive and opportunity. It is not so much different when it comes to elites and risky new technology. For elites not to block technology they need incentives, and for them to be able to foster it they need the means.

Let's talk incentives first. Elites that are in acute fear of being overthrown by internal foes (be those followers or fellow members of the elite) have a rather short time horizon for their planning. Investing into ventures such as new technology that pays off far in the future is not on their mind. What you do in such cases is plundering and stashing wealth away.

Elites that feel internally secure can afford a longer planning horizon. But they will still be conservative as outlined above. What makes them accept the risks posed by new technology is a yet greater risk: if you are threatened by an external foe, your calculus changes. Conquest and subjugation by a foreign elite and their followers is a much worse outcome than a bit of managed upheaval due to new technology. Note, however, that the perceived risk of defeat must be palpable. Large empires that are merely fighting smaller neighbours do not count. Similarly sized countries fighting or potentially fighting each other do. A country suddenly threatened by a technologically more advanced foe does too.

And then there is the question of means: technological change requires a certain scale of society, which furnishes investable resources, as well as access to key inputs, such as coal reserves for instance back in the 19th century.

Do we have data to back up this murder framework? First, we need to acknowledge that we have only very few observations to go by so this is anecdotal and suffers from what is called survivorship bias. The Neolithic Revolution happened against the backdrop of a very weak hunter gatherer elite and so does not hold many clues. The Industrial Revolution happened first in England and then with a time lag elsewhere, cases we shall review below. We have more data if we look at the general policies of states outside of these two technological revolutions to see whether the degree to which they encourage technological change correlates with this framework. In what follows we start there by doing a tour de force review of the time before 1900.

(3) A prisoners' dilemma

Innovation and technological change start in the minds of people. And the more minds there are, the more chances of ideas. The more these minds can meet and exchange and challenge ideas, the more and the better these ideas become. And the more dead minds can still tell of their ideas and findings to posteriority through writing and other cultural traditions the more the minds of the day can stand on the shoulders of giants.

It is no accident that technological development is concentrated across the globe in areas where there are many people that can mingle and talk and who have a rich cultural history to learn from. The more sparsely populated continents like America and Australia in pre-colonial times were clearly behind the curve in terms of technology. The Americas entered the Iron Age only after Columbus arrived, and Australia experienced its Neolithical Revolution only through European settlers. Africa is a very interesting continent, being both the birthplace of humanity and the birthplace of one of the earliest Neolithic revolutions in Ancient Egypt. Why did not technology develop faster in this 'oldest' home continent of ours? I would argue that its natural resources and geographic setup was not conducive to large and interconnected areas of high population density supported by agriculture. Much of the landmass is either desert, tropical rainforest, or of a dry continental temperate climate – so prime arable land was and is limited. And transportation, and with that interconnectedness, was limited by the average distance of any point of land from the nearest coastline being high and the lack of navigable rivers (except for the Nile and the Congo. And the latter didn't connect to arable land).

This leaves us with Eurasia, and the Fertile Crescent, Western Europe, the Indian subcontinent, and Eastern China as the primary population centres based on large scale productive agriculture as areas with the means to drive technological change. Now, during what times did these areas drive technological change based on these means? During times of extensive and existential conflict.

The high point of inventiveness in ancient Greece is associated with the time of the most intense competition between its city states and the struggle for survival as independent entities against the onslaught of the Persian Empire. The Parthenon that millions flock to modern day Athens to admire was build a few decades after the city had been razed to the ground by the troops of Xerxes the Great. Compare this with the inventiveness of ancient Greece during the centuries of it being a peaceful province of the Roman Empire.

Or take ancient China. Rapid advances in military technology, statecraft and the economy are generally associated with the Autumn Spring, Warring States and the Song dynasty times. All of which feature existential struggles against other societies. As an aside, and of course this is highly speculative, but had the Song dynasty not been destroyed by the Mongols, perhaps it would have entered the virtuous circle that England entered in the late 18th century. After all they had taken many steps that were prevalent in the early industrialisation stages of Europe from large scale trade flows and pre-industrial manufacturing to stock corporations for capital raising, coupled with technological breakthroughs such as printing with movable letters and gunpowder. Times of calm on the other hand, in which the elite felt externally secure were times of slow progress, with greater focus on the arts and trade as in the Tang dynasty, and even rejection of exploration and scuttling of new technologies as when the Ming emperors shut down the Treasure Voyages (a decision whose parallel would have been Spain aborting the colonisation of the Americas in the 1520s after the conquest of the Aztek Empire) or when Qing emperor Qianlong in 1793 wrote to George III of England "our Celestial Empire possesses all things in prolific abundance and lacks no product within its own borders. There was therefore no need to import the manufactures of outside barbarians in exchange for our own produce." Both these last two examples need to be placed in context, however: At the time of abandoning the Treasure Voyages, Ming China had lost Vietnam and a Ming emperor had been briefly held captive by Mongols; there were good reasons to cut back on expensive exploration. At the same time there was no existential struggle that would have made the elites desperate to find new sources of might and wealth. Same with Qianlong, he is said to have had a clear view of the technological advancement of the English, and he permitted limited trading, but he was far from desperate to catch up technologically. The long lull of the Qing empire made China lose out on the critical time period that saw England and the West industrialise.

What about the other pre-eminent population and technology centre in Asia, which is the Indian subcontinent? Here too, we see periods of intense competition alternate with periods of high centralisation and external security. And in what turned out to be pivotal centuries between 1500 and 1900, most of modern-day India was ruled by the Mughal empire to arguably similar effect as the Qing Empire in China. And then, by the time the Indian elites could have woken up to the existential threat coming from Britain they had either been co-opted by the British or defeated. And when industrialisation in England was in full swing, the British elite made sure not to have new technology flow to India, rather the opposite: focusing the Indian economy on raw material production.

And going full circle back to Europe, Roman conquest and the safety of its empire can be argued to have also let to a lull. As an interesting aside, as the Eastern half of the Roman Empire survived the Barbarian onslaught of the European Migration Period in the form of the Byzantine Empire, the latter did experience existential struggles and was perhaps more inclined to allow technological experimentation and social mobility. Perhaps they lacked the scale, and luck.

In very simplistic terms, the ensuing Middle Ages were about rediscovering the technological finesse and rebuilding the population densities that were lost during the Migration Period. Near the end of that catch up period, starting in the 15th century, great scientific and geographical discoveries were driven by societies whose elites were in intense competition with other societies: such as Spain which was driving its Reconquista from the Moors to its conclusion, and the Northern Italian city states. The latter illustrate that an outwards and trade focussed orientation of value generation of the elites acts as a further catalyst to induce technological innovation.

Europe in the Modern era resembled a classical Prisoners' Dilemma, in that the elites of the major countries would have arguably preferred a coordinated peace between one another so as to enjoy the riches of their lands and to not worry about new technologies - but were forced to move forward for fear of others moving forward and taking over one's land.

That the decisive break throughs took place in England in the end, on the periphery rather than in one of the larger states on the Continent, is somewhat surprising. It may well be an accident so to speak, but it may also have been made possible to happen because the two major population centres on the Continent (France and Germany) were weakened in their capacity by internal strife (as in the run up to the French Revolution and the ensuing chaos) or external calamity (as in the devastation of the German lands wrought by the Thirty Years war which arguably retarded developments by a century or two). As in the case of the Italian Renaissance city states, Britain was outward oriented and trade dependent – and in great competition with the Dutch in trade. And then think back to our friends the Darcy's and the existential struggle of England's elite with Napoleon against the backdrop of having been through the Seven Years' War, the world's first global war, within living memory. The English elite felt they could not afford to let go of any advantage that could be gained by a technological edge.

With these examples I have tried to cover all potential candidates for the Industrial Revolution. Stil, one may argue that the narratives tied to them are not falsifiable. And yet, all the components of the narratives can be quantified (outward orientation as percentage of income from trade and tributes for instance), and put to test against alternatives.

(4) Catch up investment

Having done our quick run through history up until the Industrial Revolution, it is also instructive to review what types of societies caught up and industrialised later.

The elites of Native American and of pre-colonial African states may have wondered about how to catch up technologically with the European conquistadores, but they were not given enough time to launch proper attempts. Indian elites may have wondered but they were prevented from acting by the British. Chinese elites launched half-hearted attempts in the 19th century but didn't succeed. The case of Japan is different.

In the early 1850s, American warships under Commodore Perry forced the Japanese government to acquiesce to opening trading relationships with the United States (and later other powers friendly with the US). These agreements came to be known as the 'Unequal Treaties', as they bestowed disproportionate benefits and influence on the Western countries.

The difference between samurai warriors clad in armour, and clutching arrows, pikes and swords, supported by a few musketeers, with the American warship sporting long range and large calibre cannons and crossing oceans by way of steam engines must have been stark. And it must have been obvious to clear-minded members of the Japanese elite that without catching up on these technologies they and their descendants would stand no chance against military aggression and economic extortion.

In reaction, a coalition of Japanese elite members conspired to change their societal setup and to embrace Western industrial technology. They successfully replaced the incumbent (shogun) leader with the emperor leader. Since the office of the emperor as ceremonial figurehead had existed for centuries, this may have looked like an inconsequential palace intrigue. But it was anything but.

Note that the shogunate elite was a classical feudal society. The shogun lived off the taxes he levied on the peasants on his 'personal lands' while the majority of land and peasants paid taxes to their respective local lord. These lords in turn owed military services to the shogun (plus additional in-kind tributes like some forced labour of their peasants). Note that this value extraction setup left the central government of the shogun with no incentives to foster industry across the country. It would not have received any taxes from the industrialists.

The new elite coalition in charge, centred on the emperor Meiji who lent his name to the regime change, embarked on a sweeping reform of the societal setup. Anything that stood in the way of acquiring and adopting new technology was done away with: they broke the privileges of the Samurai and directed a large chunk of them towards employment in new government administrations, they standardised language and currency, they sent people to learn crafts and technology abroad as well as invited foreign experts in. They had the motive or incentives and, sitting on top of a sizeable country that, unlike India and China, had been and was being largely left alone by major powers, also the opportunity or means.

Closer to the homeland of industrialisation, France and Germany were also playing catch up as they saw the balance of power shifting in favour of England. What a change compared to the agony that Napoleon had put the English elite into just a few decades earlier.

The case of the Wilhelmine German Empire is instructive. The main driver and beneficiary of industrialisation was Prussia which, at the onset of the diffusion of industrial technologies, happened to be the most centrally managed large German state with exploitable coal reserves. Outward orientation, a strong sense of vulnerability as a strong but far from dominant power in the middle of Europe (the German states had been overrun by France at the beginning of the century), fostered risk taking appetite by the elites. Investments into enabling infrastructure, breaking the Prussian lower rank landed nobility's (the 'Junkers') hold on labour mobility, transition of power to the central imperial administration with a new democratic Reichstag as a constraining force to integrate the new quasi-elites and to protect the existing elite. Mind you, this democracy did not come out of the street revolution of 1848 but out of power pooling negotiations of the old nobility in Versailles in 1871. And the nobility moved to co-opt and integrate these newly rich through welcoming them into the ranks of the nobility (think for instance Werner Siemens becoming Werner von Siemens) and through the integrative force of being reservist officers of the army.

Catch-up industrialisation, or catch-up technological leaps in general, are much easier for elites to embark upon. The potential value generation and also the societal risks and side-effects are much better understood, and this lower uncertainty makes the trade-offs in terms of investments, power dilution due to new elite members and potential lost privileges better to justify and to rally elite coalitions around. The pull factor of the opportunities offered by the new technology is thus clearer and stronger. At the same time the push factor of competition with other elites is also higher, as those elites that already possess and leverage the new technological opportunities may more easily outcompete or suppress the elite that is contemplating embarking on the technological leap.

We can think of the process to make catch-up change happen as a step-by-step iterative process, "crossing the river by feeling the stones" as the saying has it. But making a break with the past and embarking on the journey is typically better described as a single decision by a small coalition of elite members who concentrate sufficient power to force the necessary changes on the full group of elite members.

Above, we had a quick look at the coalitions around emperors Komei and Meiji in Japan, around the Wilhelmine German emperors and Otto von Bismarck. They are typical in that they come shortly after coup d'etats where a new small coalition of elites concentrates power and has the ability to make dramatic cuts against the interests of other elite members. Other similar examples Alexander II's Russia, Stalin's Soviet Union, Deng Xiaoping's China, Augusto Pinochet's Chile, Park Chung Hee's South Korea, Chiang Kai-Shek's Taiwan, Lee Kuan Yew's Singapore. Even the American industrialisation somewhat fits this pattern: Abraham Lincoln's Federal Government, through the Civil War, executed a coup d'etat of the South and ushered in the Gilded Age.

This is not surprising. While figuring out (or rather 'stumbling upon') industrialisation for the first time in England was an exercise under high uncertainty that required lots of tinkering and exploration, catching up on industrialisation was an exercise under much lower uncertainty and thus geared towards exploitation.

Exploring the unknown favours a more decentral setup of parallelised efforts, some of which will work while most will fail. Exploiting the known favours a more centralised setup of synchronised efforts. Synchronised efforts are interdependent, and that means the chances of success of each effort increase the more the other efforts are successful – while on the flipside the returns on all efforts suffer when one effort fails. At extreme levels of synchronisation, every single effort has to succeed for anything to work, as in the Anna Karenina principle of Leo Tolstoy's and Jared Diamond's.

Where detailed planning is reliable, centralised and synchronised approaches win over decentralised and parallelised approaches. Where the uncertainty is too high for such planning, they lose. It is therefore natural to find catch-up industrialisation associated with the more centralised power structures outlined above.

As an aside, in a manner mirroring fractal geometry, the level of uncertainty dictates the winning organisational structures also on lower-level organisations such as industries and companies.

Catch-up industrialisation did not happen in societies whose elites would have had to give up substantial benefits and privileges of an essentially agrarian setup and/or whose elites saw low chances of success in industrialising. These two complications can arise even before the murder motive and murder opportunity discussed above comes into play.

Countries with very low levels of urbanisation (and a correspondingly dominant share of peasants among the commoners) for instance struggled unless a highly centralised elite coalition got into power (as outlined in the examples above). The incentives of the elite to simply extract the maximum value out of pliant peasants and not bother with manufacturing and factory workers can be overwhelming. Eastern Africa and Southern Asia illustrate this. Democratic political structures inherited from colonial times could not change this dynamic.

India in the first forty or so years of its independence is also case in point: incumbent local landed elites successfully delayed improvements to labour mobility and internal trade pushed by the central government elites whose value flows depended on broader economic activity; and the Southern states with around twice the rate of urbanisation did so less and saw industrialisation kick off faster.

(5) The long shadow of technology

Like you and I, dear reader, elites have limited foresight. And second and third order effects of shifting to new technology foundations for one's value flows can be dramatic. In the beginning we quipped that the Darcys would have had no clue where England would end up in the 20th century given their support for the early industrialists in stamping out the Luddite uprisings.

In hindsight, we discern a certain pattern of these effects. Successful industrialisation substantially increased the higher share of manufacturing profits in the income of the elite. Coalitions of elite members whose income comes from industry became more powerful than coalitions of landed elites. There was thus a certain positive feedback loop for industrialisation: the better it worked, the more the society became geared towards its continued success.

And as general pattern, in societies that started out as autocracies, the new manufacturing elites eventually saw themselves better protected and better served by democratic decision-makers than by autocratic ones. Why is this? The elite is broader and has more members than before, individual fortunes can change faster. These more diffuse and shifting interests of the full elite make it harder for the feudal structure of classical autocratic central governments to co-opt these elite members to their rule. Manufacturing coalitions typically prefer bureaucratic governments. And one focal bureaucratic government form is democracy. Industrialising countries thus exhibited a tendency to become more democratic over time. We saw this in 19th century Britain and Germany, in 19th and 20th century America, and also in 20th century South Korea.

Importantly, even when genuine democracy arises not step by step but as a result of popular revolt, I would caution to interpret these revolts as successful "by the people for the people revolutions". These revolts succeed because the elite does not coordinate to put them down. The manufacturing coalitions in the elite welcome them expecting a better deal. In the 20th century this was likely not only driven by the preference for bureaucratic and thus somewhat more meritocratic selection of officials (over selection by personal connections of feudal autocracies such as the Soviet Union) – but also by the expectation that the large section of the population we introduced above as 'quasi-elites' (people in professional services for instance) would act and vote in accordance with the interests of the manufacturing coalitions.

This leads us to an interesting and important sidenote. The societal setup and political structure of a society is basically always in some manner or form sanctified. It is ideology, the signs of belief in which become shibboleths for being part of the society. Most of us do not feel this ideological indoctrination because it is so pervasive. Our brains may even be evolutionarily wired to seek conformity of thinking in terms of fundamental values and concepts of whatever society we grow up into and live in. Ideology is arguably one of the oldest organisational techniques to lower the cost of coordination among society members. Being firm in ideology is very useful: It builds cohesion among the believers, focuses minds on what is deemed important ideologically, aligns thoughts and actions, and makes coherent policy cheaper to implement. Ideological societies thus tended to outcompete and destroy non-ideological societies.

But embarking on technological change can bring second and third order effects in this realm too. Elites need to take good care to not let ideology achieve a life of its own and become a target in its own right. Being firm in ideology makes you rigid. To be useful, ideology must impose guardrails on thinking and actions. And these same guardrails can turn from useful to dangerous when circumstances shift. What used to be good, aligned policy and a high chance tactic in one world can be fatal in another. Look at armies: marching straight in formation, acting as one body in firing salvo after salvo was possibly the best guardrail on the behaviour of soldiers in the times of Napoleon. This successful military doctrine or training or ideology would have been a catastrophic mistake in World War I. Perhaps one can argue that the massed infantry assaults seen in that war were an ideological hangover from the 19th century.

The problem is compounded if successive leaders start to believe their own propaganda. This can happen because they have inherited the propaganda apparatus from their predecessors with being instructed only on their superficial working and their ideology, or this may happen because they are less experienced and less shrewd. And generally speaking, the more rigid an ideology the greater the risk that subsequent leaders and generations misinterpret it as a resource or value to be protected rather than as a tool or instrument to be used, adapted and in doubt discarded. Look at the Ottomans and the Manchu in the late 19thcentury, at the Soviet Union in the 70s (and a lot more controversially, perhaps also look at the United States in the present day).

We see here again the pattern of highly synchronised efforts being very effective in the opportunity environment for which they were designed while being very off and harmful in other environments; while decentral, loosely aligned efforts are less effective at exploiting opportunities yet more resilient in the face of changing environments. Ideology synchronises.

If we want to understand what ideologies work and what ideologies do not, we need to look at the technological opportunities and how clear the way to exploit them are. if we want to forecast how the dominant ideologies are going to change in the future, we need to understand how technological progress impacts the relative costs and benefits of different ideologies.

And as a quick, practical take-away: Don't believe your own propaganda.

It is now time to review the big technological breaks in our history and the impact they had on our organisational setup.

Chapter 3: Technology and political organisations

"The workmen desire to get as much, the masters to give as little as possible. [...] It is not, however, difficult to foresee which of the two parties must, upon all ordinary occasions, have the advantage in the dispute, and force the other into a compliance with their terms. [...] In the long run the workman may be as necessary to his master as his master is to him; but the necessity is not so immediate."
Adam Smith, 1776

Technology is a big word. And we shall use it to mean the big things. Not the bells and whistles engineering and fine-tuning, but the stuff that fundamentally changes the human condition. And that you will see, dear reader, has everything to do with costs and prices:

(1) The nature of technological shifts: solving old problems in a much cheaper way

For our purposes, it will be useful to differentiate between the following two types of inventions: one is making new things possible, like sending people to the moon with rockets, while the other is getting known things done more cheaply, such as copying books using a printing press rather than ink and pen.

Our general imagination is of course preoccupied with the first category. After all, compared to our ancestors a mere one hundred years ago, we now have airplane travel, computer games and smartphones, we send rockets to space and so on. But it is the second category that changes history.

Look at the printing press of Gutenberg's: we could copy books and leaflets before the printing press, but it was super expensive. With printing we could do such ephemeral things as newspapers. Would science, enlightenment and everything else been possible with books and equations being copied by hand letter by letter? I doubt it. The steam engine didn't do anything new that water mills and horse drawn mills couldn't already do; all they did was keep a rotating shaft turning. Locomotives and trains didn't enable something new that horse drawn carriages or oxcarts couldn't do. But steam engines and trains did these things much more efficiently, much cheaper. The critical inventor contributing to the steam engine's success, James Watt, is not known for inventing the engine per se, he is known for having improved its efficiency by a smarter way of disposing of the spent steam.

You may well be thinking that the key change of these inventions was not lower cost but higher scale – but that's having it backwards. The reason we didn't create books and newspapers at scale or moved goods and people at scale before these new technologies is not that because it would not have been technically possible, it is because it would have been prohibitively expensive.

There is a multitude of examples showing just how much humans can accomplish with basic technology of low efficiency. The great pyramids of ancient Egypt show what large structures you can build with minimalist technology if only you are willing and able to put in the effort. We stand in front of them in awe because later rulers were not able or willing to muster the enormity of resources to recreate similar feats.

Impressive as they are, the grand pyramids thus also stand for a technological dead end. They were simply too expensive to build to become a widely adopted technology. The real technological breakthroughs come with making known things in a cheaper way; they come from basics becoming cheaper, much cheaper, than before.

While there have been many breakthroughs, there have only been three revolutions thus far. Let us run quickly through them.

The advent of agriculture did not create a fundamentally new output. Our ancestors were able to feed themselves just fine with the food they got from hunting and foraging. The impact of agriculture was that the rate at which a peasant could produce food was much higher than the rate at which a hunter gatherer could produce food, while the amount of land that went into the process was much smaller. Food thus became considerably cheaper in terms of labour and space expended. This meant that higher population numbers could be sustained in more confined spaces. And through such cheap food follow-on innovation was made possible that included things we today regard as fundamental: villages, later cities, writing and mathematics, professional soldiers and scientists.

The industrial revolution is also best understood as being about harnessing a new, cheaper form of energy. The early applications of industrialisation were not about new use cases at all. They were about challenges like pumping water out of mines, and about the weaving of textiles - both of these had well-functioning solutions based on animal and human labour. The outputs of the early industrial revolution could also be produced without industrialisation. The difference was that the energy used in the process came not from muscles but from coal being burnt in steam engines. And that was a lot cheaper, especially if energy could be applied at large scale.

Let's also remember that the first locomotives were not much faster than traditional forms of transport using horses. But being able to extract energy from cheap coal at a high scale and reliably made them superior. Of course over time, we have learned new use cases that became possible because energy was becoming so cheap. And so eventually, we learned to build steam ships, we learned to turn coal into electricity and light up our homes in the evening and send telegraph messages around the world.

The third and last revolution is the information technology revolution. And it is playing out this pattern as well. The Saturn V rocket sending the first humans to the moon was designed mostly based on calculations done by people with their brains and analogue tools. It was an eminently successful process, but a rather costly one. Calculations made by a computer are much faster, more reliable and a lot cheaper than calculations made by hand. Emails, texts, videos sent over the Internet are faster, cheaper and more reliable than those sent by post, but we could send all of those communications without the help of computers. Here as well, over time, we figured out use cases and applications that were not possible without information technology. Some of the marvels of artificial intelligence do open up new frontiers, as when computers are now able to play games like chess and go at levels far beyond any human player. But here too the main application thus far is for the computer to stand in for a regular human in playing against the human user of a programme. Which is an old challenge getting a new and cheaper solution.

Deep technological shifts come not from new use cases, they come from the cheaper provisioning of fundamental, broadly used goods, such as food, energy, communication - and thinking. We had better think of the big and decisive technological breakthroughs coming from the adoption, some would say diffusion, of technologies that make basic inputs to a great many of economic processes much cheaper.

Going through history we find many examples of technological development that came about as a response to directives and requests of the society in question. The cycles are very fast when it comes to war: during the Second World War, new technologies like sonar and decryption were developed by the Allies as a direct response to the threat posed by German submarines. The Manhattan Project culminating in the development of the nuclear bomb likewise came out of a government directive. In the decades following the war, the space race between the US and the Soviet Union and the landing on the moon were likewise the fruits of 'directed technological development'. We can reach deep into the past to see similar developments happening: The mathematical and organisational feats required to build the pyramids were, at least in part, the result of the needs created by the mandate to build these monuments.

It is thus very tempting to look at technology as something that society develops to meet certain needs or to overcome certain challenges. Both in terms of technology needed for the political system to function, such as in developing voting machines and the statistics of polling and voter surveys, as well as in developing technologies in general terms, such as better weapons, more efficient industrial production methods and medical treatments of formerly untreatable diseases.

But the mantra of 'social organisations bring about new technology' is only one half of the story. It is equally true that 'technology brings about new social organisations'. These two processes run in parallel, but at different time scales.

Over shorter time horizons, it is societies developing technology in a directed manner. Over longer time horizons, it is the broad-brush adopted technology bases, the breakthroughs of cheaper food and cheaper energy that we went through above that appear to select the appropriate societal setup. The technology 'appears' to do so because, of course, it does not do so in any purposeful manner. The dynamic is a simple evolutionary process or natural selection process: societal setups that make efficient use of the opportunities offered by the prevalent technology tend to outcompete societies that do not, amassing resources, displacing other societies and inducing imitation by other societies.

Looking at the foundational technologies of agriculture, bronze smelting, iron smelting, gun powder use, steam engines, electricity – societies that leveraged them tended to outcompete those that did not.

Since the advent of agriculture about ten thousand years ago, hunter gatherers were increasingly displaced by farmers and herdsmen and pushed back to the marginal and difficult to access lands in places like Southern Africa, the Amazon and part of the Southeast Asian islands.

Over the last five hundred years, European nation states have to large part displaced social structures with inferior technology – be it basically wholesale as in the Americas, Africa, Australia and Siberia or by subjugating and co-opting existing local elites as, for instance, in India.

The actual history of these displacements is of course a lot more complex than technological superiority. At the same time, it is hard to imagine an alternative run of history in which societies with less efficient base technologies systematically outcompete societies with more efficient base technologies. Cheap food, cheap tools, cheap energy, and so on, translate into advantages through a myriad of direct and indirect ways.

And the picture that emerges thus is that more efficient baseline technologies outcompete less efficient baseline technologies, leveraging, if you will, human societies to have them spread and adopted more widely.

In the short run, societies develop and leverage application technologies to solve the problems of their day. In the long run, base level technologies leverage societies to spread themselves. This is why we should call the development of societies and technology a 'co-evolution'. This means social organisations bring about new technology and at the same time new technology brings about new social organisations.

And in this co-evolution, societies are not just actors, their very setup and structure evolves in response to new technology. This is as fascinating as it is alien to the thinking of most people, possibly also to you dear reader.

We turn now to how base level technology selects organisational structures. Importantly, there were only very few ruptures in our history where baseline technology was exchanged for a new much cheaper technology. Only the above three revolutions (cheap food, cheap energy, and cheap thinking) really moved the needle. And whenever this happened our politics and societal setup changed profoundly. And we shall get started with how the balance of power between leaders and followers in societies is impacted by the dominant base layer technologies.

Let's get started.

(2) Our starting point: two-legged large apes in the African plain

We have long known that humans are social animals. We are born into family groups, and we naturally grow up to be members of larger social groups. Our ability use language for communication is in all likelihood a hardwired capability of our brains that we inherit from our ancestors. Children have a window of language learning in their early years during which they pick up the languages around them seemingly without effort and without flaws.

This is not surprising if we look at our closest relatives, the chimpanzees. They live in social groups of typically a few dozen members. Their subsistence is based on hunting and gathering which they do in a cooperative manner. Coordination is achieved through elaborate communication. And joint decision-making is made easier by dominance structures, one per gender. They are territorial, defending their hunting and foraging grounds against other groups. Some groups engage in warfare as well, which sees expeditions formed, made up of male members, that attack other groups with lethal force. The primary objectives are conquering territory and abducting females, arguably the two main resources of a chimpanzee group.

In stripping branches of their leaves and bark to be used as a sort of fishing rods for termites, chimpanzees can be said to leverage technology. They pass down the know-how of such technology through generations via demonstration and imitation. This induces cultural variation between groups in that some technologies are discovered and retained by some groups, but not by others.

Similar to chimpanzees, every social group of humans has leaders and followers. Social groups would not yield much benefit to their members if the actions of theirs were not coordinated and the resource allocation not clarified. This is done by the leadership. Leadership means many things, but in essence it is about steering the coordination of followers and the sharing of the spoils.

While mechanisms can be constructed in theory that enable members of a group to coordinate their actions and split resources without the need of leadership, we have not seen any such mechanism work out well enough in practice to be a serious contender to leadership-led groups.

Human hunter gatherer social organisations are similar to those of chimpanzees: a small band of families that live, work and move around together. Members know each other individually, the levels of differentiation between members in terms of skills and tasks is relatively low, and leadership is based on a combination of trust and fear between individuals. Judging from hunter gatherer people that have survived into modern times, these groups can but need not be combined into larger hierarchies of tribes and chieftainships that coordinate, particularly vis-à-vis other such larger organisations.

It is important to note at this point the pressure that evolution puts on leaders in terms of how to split the spoils. If you are the leader, then you have to choose where to place your group on the line between you being extremely selfish and retaining everything for yourself and you being extremely altruistic and starve rather than take anything for yourself. Leaders whose genes make them more likely to decide at either of the two extremes are unlikely to be successful and leave children behind, for obvious reasons. But the optimal point is not a goldilocks egalitarianism either. The optimal point is the answer to being selfish with restraint: the leader taking as much for him- or herself as possible while not running too high a risk of being ousted by rebellion. Genes that drive their carriers to this point outcompete genes that drive to another point.

Throughout history, we should thus expect leaders to be selfish to the point of almost endangering their position by squeezing their followers of resources. This, again, is true of both chimpanzees as humans.

The next big question of course is what determines the risk of being ousted by rebellion. In economic terms, leaders and followers are bargaining over the spoils of working together. While there are many factors, three of them stand out in our story.

- The first one is how easily and how well the leader can direct, monitor and judge the work and effectiveness of the followers;
- the second is how easily and how well the followers can retaliate against the leaders when they are disgruntled;
- and, taking a step back, the third one is how closely the preferences and incentives of the leader and follower are aligned in the minds of the follower. If the follower trusts the leader to essentially act on his behalf, then he will be more willing to follow orders, endure hardship and make sacrifices.

These three factors influenced the bargaining position of leader and follower in prehistoric times, and they have been influencing them all the way to the present day. When factory workers go on strike and demand higher pay, when children bargain with their parents overcompensation for mowing the grass, when people gather in the streets to protest an unjust policy or regime – these three factors are at play and help us understand how strong the bargaining position of the respective leaders and followers are.

So as we pick this apart for our hunter gatherer forebears, compare this in your mind to present day such bargaining. Factor one: leaders can more easily check on the work of the followers:

- Imagine the group of hunters on the hunting trail: they are spending the whole day together and very clearly see and observe what everyone else is doing.
- And the skill and knowledge of the follower is clearly observable. When forming a piece of flintstone into a stone knife, the precise and seemingly effortless movements of the worker showcase the skill and the experience.

- The time lag between effort expended and the outcome is short. Compare the immediate gratification that a successful hunt affords with the societal payoff of basic research in a lab which may materialise only decades later.
- Outcomes are easily measurable, as in the number of arctic hares captured or in the size of the mammoth slain. And in case the prey got away, the counterfactual can be intuitively constructed and is obvious to everyone in the group.

And followers can more easily retaliate the more of the below points are true:

- First of all, the above points mean also that followers can easily judge the merits of the leader and observe how he or she split the spoils, i.e. what kind of deal he was giving them.
- Next, in case the followers felt they could get a better deal, they could individually or in coalition groups challenge the leadership role of the leader and claim it for themselves. When followers can easily coordinate their actions amongst themselves such coalitions can emerge with fewer obstacles.
- And then the decision to challenge the leadership is easier if the retaliation against the leader can be actioned quickly, and the effects felt by the leader without much delay, as well as if the followers can ratchet the pressure on the leader easily up and down and also stop the pressure without having inflicted lasting damage on themselves or the leader. All these characteristics of conflict make for a quick and relatively painless conflict, in short: a low-risk conflict.

As for aligned preferences, followers will trust the benevolence of the leader more if some of the following is true:

- There is a shared kinship between the leader and the followers. Hunter gatherer groups were extended family groups, and so kin selection was clearly hard at work in their evolution.
- In modern societies, we also see this in the form of resources going into common goods that benefit all rather than into private consumption of the leader. This can take the form of basic infrastructure, mutual insurance, religious rites and constructions. A special case of this is the rallying around the flag: There is a common enemy, an alien and threatening organisation prevailing against which is in the intense interest of all and being defeated by is an intense anguish for all.

It is clear that back then the role of a leader was made easy by being part of the team at work and by being fairly familiar with everything that the members of the group would be doing. Coordination and efficiency of decision-making were thus likely rather high.

When it came to splitting the spoils, the pressure towards a roughly egalitarian distribution was high as both leader and followers were highly enabled to retaliate against each other in case of being disgruntled with the deals they were getting. And on top, if the follower did not agree with the leader but was not able to challenge him or her, then leaving the group and joining another was arguably a very real option. Voting with their feet if you wish.

Life was harsh for sure, but it was also egalitarian and possibly came also with a fair bit of leisure time.

(3) The first break: cheap food

Hunter gatherer times cover over 90% of the time that humans have lived on earth. And in about 95% of the remainder of this time humans lived in agrarian societies which came about in the so-called Neolithic Revolution.

This revolution denotes the invention and adoption of agriculture. That yielded more food and thus supported higher levels of population, allowed specialists to work on things unrelated to food production, the creation of tools and weapons made of metal, the formation of cities and of professional armies.

Cheap food has enabled amazing things through scaling the number of humans on Earth. We do not know these numbers yet precisely, but there were no more than something like a few dozen million people alive at any point in time before the advent of agriculture. Fast forward fifty to a hundred generations and you find individual states that encompassed as many people. Hunter gatherer groups coming together occasionally for trading and other business get to perhaps a few thousand people being in close proximity. Compare that to the large cities of antiquity with hundreds of thousands of inhabitants.

And with the number of people come the number of inventive and inquisitive brains. There is not a single hunter gatherer society that would be literate, not a single hunter gatherer society that has figured out the usage of metal. The large corpuses of culture that the great civilisations of today look back on have all been enabled by the cheap food that fed our ancestors in the past few thousand years.

Agriculture also significantly changed the bargaining power between leaders and followers. As we move from hunter gatherers to agrarian societies, we can move from 'followers' to 'peasants' and from 'leaders' to 'elites'. The latter is to mark the change of the personal leadership of the small egalitarian bands to the hierarchies with multiple layers and different types of roles that together form the leadership of successful agrarian societies of many thousands of members.

The key thing to note is that in a predominantly agricultural economy, leadership and the elite need not be particularly responsive to the needs of the masses. As long as there are subsistence level resources for followers plus a strong public administration apparatus the elite is fine. The reason for this is that peasants cannot fight back against leaders other than through outright rebellion or emigration.

The threshold to enter outright rebellion is high; it is very risky undertaking after all. And certainly so once bronze weapons had emerged. Very few peasant revolts in history have succeeded. Looking for instance at the circa four millennia of Chinese history with about twelve major dynasties, we know of two significant peasant revolts that succeeded in overthrowing the regime. What these outliers then brought about was not, however, a peasant utopia but rather an exchange of the former leadership with the leaders of the rebellion (the Han and the Ming dynasties).

Critically, low level revolt in the sense of resisting small demands, of not putting in the whole effort, of silent quitting and so on does not work well in an agrarian setup. Not paying taxes is difficult because the harvest can be gauged reliably with low effort by the local elite. Not doing work as in being on strike is also of no use: it is either ineffectual, as in the wheat on the field continuing to grow whether the peasant is on strike or not, or it is economically fatal, as in not feeding one's livestock and seeing it starve to death or not bringing in the harvest in time and risk seeing a year's worth of work and subsistence be lost to the vagaries of nature.

Going through the list of bargaining factors we reviewed above, there is one last way out for peasants: moving to another group, voting with their feet. Alas, this option is also more easily curtailed by the elite compared to hunter gatherer times. Throughout antiquity, we read of variants of indentured peasants and slaves – no matter what geographical or cultural region we look at. Agrarian societies tend to severely restrict the mobility of peasants – and thereby further strengthen the bargaining power of the elite. At the extreme, mobility is reduced to zero and with that there is no market mechanism left to govern the bargaining between elite and peasant, leaving the latter the choice of "take it or die".

This raises an interesting question. While it is very clear that the average output or income per person was higher in agrarian societies than in hunter gatherer societies, was the average income of a follower / peasant also higher? To make that more concrete, imagine the peasants labouring on the fields on the banks of the river Nile during the Old Kingdom of Ancient Egypt. Their very recent ancestors had lived in the same land as hunters and gatherers. Were they better off as farmers? The scribes of the pharaoh measured and allocated land to families every year, they calculated painstakingly how much tax to pay to the pharaoh and to his temples as well as where and what do as part of compulsory labour. It may well be that for the 95% or so of ancient Egyptians who were peasants, material life actually deteriorated compared to their hunter gatherer ancestors.

This is not to say that there would not have been scope to improve their lot; after all, the Egyptian society overall became a lot more productive with cheap food at scale. And if we fast forward through the centuries, peasants of agrarian societies became clearly better off than their hunter gatherer forebears. Even if their bargaining position did not improve, they still benefited from technological progress and trade: better farming techniques like crop rotation lowered the risk of famine, new crops from far flung places brought variety to diets, better tools and farm animals made work less laborious, and so on.

And then there was of course some competition between elites over peasants which raised their bargaining position. This was visible most clearly after great epidemics when owners of fallow land were outbidding one another to get hold of peasants to work it; and after the discovery of 'pristine' land that could be colonised.

Intuitively, the natural selection of societal setups favours elite coordination mechanisms that enable elite members to fend off take-overs from rival internal elite factions / aspirants as well as external elite aspirants. Key characteristics that successful societal organisations were selected for include the following:

- First, local presence of the elite with the same person in charge of the same land over extended periods. This is helpful because land productivity is variable on the local level across both space and time and being in place enables the leadership to build the knowledge and experience to judge the harvests well to not overtax or undertax the local populace. Whether feudal lords of the manor overseeing a couple of hamlets or villages and living in close proximity or ancient Egyptian scribes overseeing a portion of the Nile bank and carefully measuring the yearly flood levels, all this was to ensure efficiently maximised taxation.
- Second, the local elite would aim to make it very hard for peasants to move away. Outside of the exceptional cases such as after epidemics, the benefit of attracting peasants away from neighbouring local elites was low. The limiting factor of producing more food was anyhow the availability of land, not the availability of peasants. What is more, the number of peasants kept growing automatically anyhow in a Malthusian fashion. Successful agrarian societies would thus tend to have low levels of labour mobility.
- Third, taxation is typically set such as to keep most of the population at the subsistence level. This maximised tax revenues without starving the workers and without risking revolt, and this also lowered the resources of peasants in case they revolted. And due to the limited retaliation options of farmers to begin with, as noted above, this is also generally feasible. We see this through all of history, including in relatively advanced societies such as the mid-20th century Soviet Union.
- Fourth, there is very little investment into the knowledge of workers. While the children of the elite are educated and trained through

> elaborate schemes and by carefully selected specialists, the calculus on peasants always landed on leaving it to learning by doing as they work together with older generations. Too much knowledge would potentially be dangerous anyhow. There is a reason that large scale and persistent religions were typically secretive towards the masses: only select few priests and elite members were allowed into the inner sanctum of Egyptian temples, sacrifice and temple work was reserved to a certain genealogical elite in both ancient Israel and India. And Catholic Christian mass was held in Latin and thus unintelligible to virtually everyone.

How was the elite itself organised? The earliest elite structures simply integrate hunter gatherer groups led by one leader each into a larger group whose leader then in turn leads the leaders of the individual groups. This is a feudal structure, and much like the leadership of a hunter gather group, it is built on personal relationships, trust in individuals, fear of individuals. Elite members aimed to maintain not only their own power, status and material well-being but also that of their children, leading to hereditary power transitions. We call these structures monarchies and aristocracies. These structures emerged essentially all over the world, and enabled by cheap food, they thoroughly outcompeted hunter gatherer groups.

With the invention of writing, contracts, laws and accounting are made possible, leading to the emergence of Weberian bureaucratic structures. These can, in principle, outcompete feudal structures because they can leverage and direct large scale resource allocations and building projects. Compared to agrarian societies outcompeting hunter gatherer societies, however, the advantage of bureaucratic societies to feudal societies is much weaker. Outcompeting has thus taken a longer period of time, and there has been an ebb and flow of the two structures in history. And while the remaining hunter gatherer societies on Earth today are relegated to the most remote and small specks of the world such as parts of the Amazon rainforest and New Guinean mountains, there are countries today that are essentially feudal in structure even though supplemented with bureaucratic elements: we find some in the broader Arab world and in Southeast Asia, perhaps also in central Asia and in parts of Africa. It is telling, perhaps, that the so-called grave of empires, Afghanistan, has retained its fundamentally feudal structure throughout all the attempts at conquest by bureaucratic empires.

But then we need to be careful in our designations. Modern societies retain a very large element of feudal structures in the form of companies and parties. Family owned and founder led companies in particular often have a strong streak of feudal structures.

And as a historical curiosity, the structural setup of the European Middle Ages can perhaps best be understood as the symbiosis (or collaboration) of feudal organisational structures, i.e. the worldly rulers in their castles, and a bureaucratic structure, the Catholic priests in their churches and palaces as well as monks and nuns the monasteries. Not surprisingly, they were often at odds and competing for resources despite their power sharing agreement: following a highly generous interpretation of the scripture ("Render unto Caesar the things that are Caesar's, and unto God the things that are God's"), the church maintained its own taxation system and its own legal system.

The European Middle Ages are also instructive in showing that illiterate people can only build command and control structures based on personal interactions and personal trust. For bureaucracies you need literacy.

And with this, we have covered 99% of our history. The first circa 100'000 years of human history our dominant organisational structure was that of small egalitarian tribes. This was followed by our recorded history, i.e. the one with writing and states – and up until about the mid-19th century this recorded history is all about agrarian societies developing, collaborating and competing; with hereditary elites, led typically by a monarch, in a feudal or bureaucratic structure directing resources from mostly agrarian supply chains.

To bring this point home, even the societal structure of revolutionary France, the epitome of the Enlightenment and modernity, would be easily understandable and relatable for Sumerian bureaucrats from 4000 years ago: swap in churches and temples of reason for the ancient Sumerian religion, translate from French to Accadian, exchange the revolutionary intelligentsia for Sumerian aristocracy, human rights and civil laws for steles of law. It would then all be recognisable: the behaviours, the power relationships, and the distribution of the workforce across types of work. Even the Reign of Terror they would have recognised as one of the usual upshots of a new elite taking over.

And what about our friends the Darcys? They dressed differently, the spoke a different language and believed in a different religion, but if you strip that away, their way of life, their everyday technology, their modes of transport, their interactions with the people around them at Pemberly and in London – they could have just as well been local elite members of Roman Britain 1700 years earlier, shuttling between their Latifundium Pemberlinium and their city house in Londinium.

(4) The second break: cheap energy

Things changed profoundly though with the Industrial Revolution, ushering in the third epoch of dominant societal structures.

It is one of the great ironies of history that the impoverishment and exploitation of workers described and decried by Marx in 1867 would turn out to be the marker of a turning point of history leading to mass welfare, mass education, and mass democracy.

He thought he was witnessing the capitalist bourgeoisie squeezing the labourers dry. Factory workers in his telling were a proletariat enslaved to the clocks that govern their waking lives and living hand to mouth while toiling away under precarious and hazardous conditions. But that is only one part of the story.

The other, bigger part of the story is about humans learning to harness cheap energy from coal, building large scale manufacturing on top of coal and this in turn shifting elite incentives towards enabling high labour mobility.

Agrarian societies mostly used muscle power as energy source: Be that in the form of horses and oxen for transport and for working the fields, or in the form of men and women in construction, and the crafts. The two important exceptions were wood for fire and the wind for sailing ships and windmills. The main reason these remained exceptions is arguably that these two energy sources could be leveraged only for very specific use cases: sails work for watercraft on large water surfaces (on narrow waters like rivers, moving heavy barges required rowers or haulers); sails are useless for land transport. Fire enables a list of important use cases like cooking, heating, smelting metals, and burning down forests and enemy towns, but that is essentially the full list. Any other use case requiring energy had to rely on muscle power.

This changed with the invention and perfection of the steam engine following the work of Newcomen and Watt in 18th century England. Feeding a steam engine coal and water puts a shaft in motion, and, with a bit of engineering, its rotation can be turned into a plethora of movements with which power-hungry process steps could be made to rest on the energy of coal rather than the energy of food through muscle.

In the early years, steam engines replaced muscle power in processes that had already been in wide use, such as in pumping water out of mines or in weaving cloths and textiles. But with energy thus becoming a lot cheaper, previously unprofitable processes in manufacturing became viable enterprises. Bridges, ships, and railroads could be made of iron and steel (imagine producing metal works at this scale leveraging an army of blacksmiths in their smithies, that would have been a nightmare to coordinate, feed, and pay).

With miniaturisation and improved reliability, the steam engine eventually became mobile, in the form of locomotives and steam ships, thereby dramatically lowering the cost of transport. And that in turn made industries viable that depended on heavy and bulky inputs from far afield places and/or needed to deliver their heavy and bulky outputs to far away customers. Further inventions opened up yet more sources of cheap energy, the most momentous of which would prove to be mineral oil, leveraged through the internal combustion engines of Otto and Diesel.

Steam engines and the machines they powered did not work on their own. They needed a lot of people to tend to them and to perform the non-automated process steps, as well as to supervise and plan the work. In other words, in order to exploit the opportunities offered by cheap energy, the elite needed factory workers. Lots of factory workers.

Whereas at the beginning of the 19th century only a low single digit percentage of the British population was engaged in manufacturing activities (while over 80% laboured as peasants), by the end of the century manufacturing employees made up over 20% of the workforce (and the share of peasants had halved to about 40%). This had profound implications for the bargaining dynamics between the elite and the commoners and therefore favoured a different societal setup with which the elite could coordinate itself.

We go through the framework we put together for hunter gatherer times above. We start with how well factory owners could check the work of workers and verify the quantity and quality of their work:

- The verification easy, cheap and reliable. Factory owners were arguably able to perform supervision in a more effective and efficient manner than the lords of the manor checking on their peasants.
- And what is more, the skill and effort level of the individual worker is less important: whereas a skilled and experienced goldsmith produces a very different quantity and quality of output compared to an apprentice of his, the output of a factory worker depends less on his skill and more on the efficiency of the machines and the stability of the rhythm with which the workers of the factory keep them humming. Output is less individual, making supervision easier for elite members.
- The feedback cycles are also shorter: you do not need to wait for a season to see and collect the fruits of your labour. Output is churned out in a near continuous stream. Even building large structures like locomotives give you near immediate interim feedback in the form of intermediate parts like the chassis, the engine, the wheels, the instruments getting ready and then coming together.

This looks like a clear win for the elite. What this also meant though is that the value generated by an additional worker was very obvious and easily calculable for the factory owner. And these return-on-investment calculations lead to stronger competition for workers between elite members.

Commoners also gained in the sense that factory workers were able to retaliate against the factory owners a lot more easily and with lower risk than peasants against their lords:

- Going on strike was effective and inflicted immediate pain on the factory owner (without their labour the factories idled, unlike acres and meadows), yet not too effective (machines do not die when not tended to for a few days unlike livestock) and could easily be calibrated up or down by ending of prolonging the strike.
- Coordination in the form of unions was also much easier to achieve. Not only did workers live and work in much closer physical proximity, talking the same language and observing each other's lot and thoughts; they also were able to measure and keep track of their effort and output more easily – much like the factory owners themselves.

Finally, in terms of perceived benevolence of the leaders by the followers, large scale industrial societies initially built on what worked in large scale agrarian societies: for most of history, the central point of allegiance and the main source of meaning beyond material wants has been based on kinship and on religion.

But concurrently to industrialisation, a new focal point of allegiance and identity developed: the nation. European monarchs had ruled 'by the grace of God', the caliphs as successors of the prophet, Chinese emperors by the mandate of heaven, the ancient Indian rulers by the esteem of their caste, while the pharaohs and the rulers of the Incas had been godlike themselves. Compare this to the patriotic fervour shining through the agents of Imperialism and the two world wars of the last century.
And finally, in the 20th century we see the emergence of genuine democracies which, by way of elections, are perceived to align the interests of followers and their political leaders. Further down, we shall also get to the question of why nationalism emerged only in the wake of the Industrial Revolution.

But first, recall that societal setups in which the elite coordinates to better take advantage of technological opportunities tend to outcompete other societal setups. For agrarian societies this was, at the base, about controlling the surplus food production of peasants and, with that secured, about gaining access to and controlling trade routes as well as military technologies and tactics.

For industrialising societies, the key challenges were different. For them to be successful, the highest order challenge was for the elite to coordinate about how to mobilise and shift commoners into manufacturing work of the emerging factories. These workers did not come out of nowhere, they came out of the pool of workers in agriculture.

It is instructive to remember that the first wave of workers in factories, in the very early stages of the Industrial Revolution in England, featured rather high proportions of women and children among them. This points to the relative underemployment of them in agriculture back then (where heavy manual labour was needed), but it also points to the lower pressure against their mobility by the established elite. Mr and Mrs Darcy wouldn't terribly mind if the underemployed young of their tenant peasants went to work in the factories of their industrialist friends, after all. Their male tenants working the fields on the other hand, that's a different story. They are needed to generate the 10'000 pounds a year...

With manufactured goods becoming so cheap, and hence the demand for them growing so fast, employment of factory workers also kept growing – outgrowing the reservoir of underemployed workers from the countryside. And that's when the real conflicts started to erupt. I am not referring to the conflict between the Luddites and the industrialists, but the conflict between the Darcys and their fellow landed aristocrats and the emerging industrial elites. With a very clear return-on-investment calculation of factory workers and competition between factories for workers, wages were growing and eventually outgrew the livelihood provided by agricultural labouring.

With that the question was whether society should (continue to) organise around personal relationships between tenants and landlords, with high barriers to movement of peasants away from their 'ancestral lands', versus to organise around market-based contractual work with wages and high labour mobility.
Given the very high return on investment of shifting commoners from agriculture to factories, coalitions of emerging industrialists and parts of the old landed aristocrats, who financed the industrialists and benefited from the taxes they paid, saw their interests better served by pushing for market-based transactions and wage-based employment. Aristocrats would have loved to keep their agricultural labourers as close as possible to hereditary servitude. But that was not possible without giving up in the promises of industrialisation.
As a sidenote, it doesn't actually matter whether the elite made these calculations or not. As long as some societies happened to adopt societal

structures that enable high labour mobility, they would be the ones building factories and outcompeting those that stuck with protecting the interests of the land-owning elite.

This is why Marx was writing about the wage-earning proletariat in in 19th century Manchester, rather than a Northern English slave kingdom based on factories. Industrialisation in England saw the birth of manufacturing cities with historically unprecedentedly rapid population growth, from London to Birmingham to Manchester. And while the living conditions in these were quite appalling, their growth is testament to both the little hindrance that peasants and agricultural labourers encountered in migrating to the cities and the pull that the cities exerted on rural populations through economic opportunity.

Well, this was the situation in the English homeland anyway. In the industrial heartland of the British Empire, high labour mobility based on wages and contracts made a lot of sense for the elite to support. Keeping labourers in conditions close to servitude in the colonies (including Ireland) was another matter. Plantations of sugar cane and cotton in the Americas for instance continued to operate with slaves well into the later waves of industrialisation, partly into times that Marx himself would no longer witness.

As an interesting thought, the American Civil War can be interpreted not as a movement for greater federal say over the states or for abolishing slavery but rather as a contest over whether the slaves of the South should continue to labour for free on cotton plantations in the South or whether they should labour for a wage in the factories of the North. And actions speak louder than words: The Civil War was indeed followed by a mass movement of former slaves to the industrial centres in the North, but it was not followed by deep reformation of the South. If it had been, we would arguably not have seen Jim Crow laws and the policies of segregation that sparked the Civil Rights movement a century later.

So, the rise of manufacturing in the Industrial Revolution led to the adoption of a wage and contract-based relationships between the elite member and the worker, away from more personal agrarian relationship that bound the worker to the soil he was working. And competition between industrialists meant wages came close to reflecting the marginal productivity of the workers, rather than something akin to a subsistence payment in most agrarian times.

Note that satisfying the interests of the workers and paying them higher wages is a byproduct of industrialisation. And yet, with a lag, this byproduct has seen a dramatic increase in the wake of the Industrial Revolution.

Let us turn to the new elite members, the industrialists; like Frank Vickerman, the friend of the Darcys. As noted above, the established, or 'incumbent' elite in successful societies accepted these "new money" elite members because their expertise and entrepreneurship brought forth ever more wealth and ever more taxes.

What kind of structural characteristics of their society did the early industrialists require to thrive? As discussed, they needed high labour mobility and wage-based employment to feed their factories. Next, we need to realise that, in contrast to immovable assets like land, manufacturing assets like factories can be moved around over the time horizon of a few years or decades. The outlook of secure property rights is thus more prominent in the decision-making and incentive structure on investments of industrialists. Being safe from arbitrary expropriation and, more generally, enjoying the rule of law hinged on an efficient and largely objective judiciary. And that in turn depended on the process by which judges were instated and promoted and new laws created. And this takes us to the crucial role of representation and veto rights in the places where new laws are created.

Now, while there are many ways to achieve peace of mind for industrialists so that they re-invest their profits, the most common early commitment device of the incumbent elite to guard against the looming threat of expropriation of the new elite members turned out to be what we can call 'bourgeois democracy'. Democracy in its early forms as in Revolutionary France, England in Napoleonic times and the United States of the founding fathers come with many caveats: it co-existed with large scale slavery, voting rights reserved for men (or even for wealthy men only), and made holding a political office a self-funded exercise, i.e. something only for the financially independent.

Involving industrialists directly in the political process had the added benefit of aligning the policies of the state with what is conducive to industry. With the incentive basics covered, the next step would be policies that made manufacturing activities easier, more profitable and able to scale: public investments into infrastructure (for transport in particular, think of the canals in early 19th century Britain and the railways in Britain, Germany and the United States in the later decades of the century), free trade and the opening of new export markets (think the Empire and the age of Imperialism) as well as stable international currency exchange ranges (think the gold standard).

As an interesting side comment, perhaps classical Athens can be viewed as an early industrial society. Its economic base can be argued was not agriculture but large-scale shipping and trading – and the trading magnates were closer in their mindset and decision-making to 19th century industrialists than to agricultural landlords. After all, ships and trading houses are very highly mobile assets. So it may be, as a historical curiosity, that the democracy of Pericles reflected an accommodation of the new money traders by the landed elite of the old aristocracy.
Likewise, the Mercantilism of the Dutch and English and other colonising powers of the 18th century foreshadow in many of their characteristics the industrial nation states a century later. In the rule of law, in the moves towards democracy, and also, as we shall see later, in their religious and philosophical outlook.

The potentially most consequential side effect of sophisticated and scaled industrialisation was mass education and the rise of the knowledge worker. This is what would take bourgeois democracy to genuine democracy.

The rise of the knowledge worker is a classic case of unintended consequences. In order to run the complex operations, legal structures and finances of an industrial economy, the elite needed ever larger numbers of highly educated specialists: think of all the accountants, lawyers, clerks, brokers, managers, controllers, etc. And this is how mass education and mass university entrances came into being. So far so intentional. What was, in all likelihood, not intentional is the political power that the newly formed large percentage of knowledge workers with good incomes turned out demanding. Knowledge is dangerous for the elite as knowledge workers, in the words of Jim Hacker of "Yes, Prime Minister", are "people who think they ought to run the country" (given many of them read the Guardian). The answer to this has been to enable knowledge workers to become 'quasi-elites' through building personal wealth out of savings. Earn enough money to be able to live off your investments and you are an entry grade elite member.

In this context, it is very easy to misunderstand the role of labour unions and of political parties representing manufacturing workers as their core constituency. Industrialists and workers were naturally engaged in intense and heated bargaining over how to split the pie, inflicting heavy losses on each other through strikes and strike-breakers. But they also had aligned incentives when it came to the large questions that their societies faced: opening up export markets, investing in public infrastructure, investing into mass education, setting up collectivised welfare (which is cheaper than the individual kind). Together, they formed a symbiotic 'manufacturing industrial complex' or 'manufacturing coalition'.

In fact, with manufacturing as the backbone of the economy, the incentives of the dominant elites, this manufacturing coalition, are very much aligned with the incentives of the workers or commoners. Looking at marginal tax rates in the region of 90% coupled with supersized public investments such as the GI Bill, the interstate highway system and the establishment of state universities, the mid-20th century American democracy likely represents the pinnacle of elite and commoner incentive alignment.

It was the requirements of the economically dominant technological opportunity of industrial manufacturing that, through this incentive alignment, brought genuine democracy and the welfare state.

In other words, the Industrial Revolution ushered in a period in which democracies coupled with market economies and a social welfare state were the dominant political structures. From constrained, bourgeois democracies with an eye on integrating the newly rich industrialists and merchants and one on committing to not expropriating their future investment returns, to mass education and the rise of the knowledge worker quasi-elites and the manufacturing coalitions, we ended up with a high degree of incentives alignment between commoners and elite and hence democracy yielded high benefits at low costs. We shall go into this in a more structured manner further below.

For now, remember that in the 20th century so great was the aura of success of democratic systems that even the German Democratic Republic and the Democratic Republic of Congo called themselves 'democratic'!

(5) The post-industrial present-day West – a preview of the third break?

After cheap food and cheap energy, the third break, cheap thinking in the form of information technology and artificial intelligence, is upon us. But it has not landed yet. Where we are today is perhaps best understood as a transitional period which blends elements of the past manufacturing dominated societal structures with elements of the societal structures that will become dominant in the future. Let's take a moment to check what the present may offer us in terms of glimpses of the future. After all, as the saying goes, the future is already here, it is just unevenly distributed.

The future is, perhaps, more present in the developed world. Not because of the effect of cheap thinking landing earlier but because the manufacturing sector has been hollowed out due to offshoring and the rise of emerging markets. With the decline of manufacturing in the developed world for the past 50 years the power of the manufacturing coalition within the elite has waned (including that of unions). Now, what has that meant for societal setups so far?

We start with labour mobility. We have seen how agriculture makes for very low labour mobility of peasants, while manufacturing makes for high labour mobility of workers. In developed economies today more than 80% of commoners work in neither of these two sectors; they work in services instead. So what is their labour mobility?

When we talk services as in 80% of the present-day workforce, it is important to note that we are not referring to the small slice of so-called professional services, the high-end lawyers, doctors, tax advisors, accountants and the like. These are the quasi-elite we talked about above. Rather, we are talking about mass scale service jobs as you find them in hospitality, retail, basic medical services, cleaning, driving etc. Now, in what sense are these service jobs different from manufacturing:

- The quantity and quality of output is less easily measurable. Output depends more fuzzily on labour input. While the market value of manufactured goods is simple to ascertain, the value of services to the end customer is revealed often only indirectly later. Cars come in a certain stable quality, branding and price buckets, being driven around in car by a taxi driver or an on-hire gig worker on the other hand can be good or bad experience that is difficult to pin down in how the transaction is measured and settled.
- This is driven by the fact that individual (soft) skills matter more in services than in manufacturing. The best conveyor belt worker out of 100 workers had a contribution that was a bit better than the average worker's, measured in percentages. The best salesperson out of 100 sales people, however, is a number of times more productive than the average sales person. And for occupations like software engineers this value contribution gap increases to orders of magnitude, i.e. ten times or a hundred times more value generated. This means of course that the labour force is less homogenous, and that commoners are less fungible across employers.
- Employers thus have an incentive to bind the good catches very closely to them while weeding out (letting go of) the lemons.
- There is a second general characteristic that comes from moving away from factories and machines: Staffing levels need not be synced meticulously with business activity. Running three more manufacturing lines without the additional workers cannot be done, running another wing of a hospital or a hotel can be done without commensurate hiring by simply lowering service and maintenance levels. Smoothing out the periods of over- and underemployment costs much less with services. The converse (too many workers) is also more benign. Instead of idling, the surplus can still create some value by increasing temporarily the service levels beyond their efficient level.

All of these points push towards a more relationship-based employment rather than transactional employment, and they all push towards less acute competition for workers between elite members. Hence the elite has a lower incentive to enhance labour mobility.

There is also a second pattern at play that comes from the enormous value gaps between the superstar software engineers and mediocre engineers, the superstar lawyers and mediocre lawyers etc. For the elite, it is much easier and cheaper to co-opt the few bright and creative top talent service workers (like software engineers) and make them 'quasi-elites' or junior members of the elite - while keeping or making general labour mobility low. Rather than solving for the total workforce, rather solve for the top few percent most productive ones.

We see characteristics and symptoms of serfdom resurfacing in the developed world, more so in some countries than in others, possibly more so in those with lower levels of manufacturing:

- Median incomes stagnate while average income keeps growing. In arcane economic speak either steady state marginal productivity and hence wages stagnate, or wages are decoupling from marginal productivity, with the latter being the more intuitive explanation. The last time we had wages not reflecting marginal productivity was in the pre-Civil War cotton plantations of the Southern United States.
- High levels of debt of commoners. This ties them down and discourages job switching while encouraging second jobs and moonlighting.
- Public services are being hollowed out: from healthcare to utilities, from transport infrastructure to public investments into education.
- At the same time, a parallel world of infrastructure and service structures is being created for the elite and quasi-elite (from private healthcare to zones with higher service utilities, from ride hailing and private jets to private schools and universities).

The incentives of the elite and the incentives of the commoners at large have clearly been diverging since the heydays of the mid-20th century.

Chapter 4: The third break, cheap thinking

邦有道，贫且贱焉，耻也；邦无道，富且贵焉，耻也。
"In a country well governed, poverty is something to be ashamed of. In a country badly governed, wealth is something to be ashamed of."
Ascribed to Confucius, about 500 B.C.

In July 2018, the Foreign Affairs magazine ran a series of essays that all aimed to answer the same question: what world are we living in? The proposed answers were a world dominated by (a) the return of great power politics, (b) the resilience of Western dominance, (c) group identities, (d) the late vindication of Marx, (e) the digital revolution, and (f) climate change.

If you take a longer-term view, there are only two serious contenders in this list, the last two. And the right answer I believe was (e), the Digital Revolution and AI. This is the third break after cheap food and cheap energy. Cheap thinking will be a lot more momentous than all the other things in that list taken together.

How momentous? Similar in magnitude to the preceding two big technological shifts. Moving from hunter gatherer times to agrarian times gave us cities, culture, civilisation – agrarian societies have history while the other ones we call prehistoric. Moving from agrarian times to industrial times gave us mass affluence, modern democracy, moon landings – industrial societies define what it is to be modern while the other ones we call pre-modern or historic. Moving from industrial to intelligent societies will be similarly epoch defining, even if our living space on planet Earth should shrink by sea levels rising 70 meters when Antarctica melts.

It is tempting to equate cheap thinking with artificial intelligence. But it is a broader phenomenon. The first calculators already made certain types of thinking cheaper, the first programmable computers made other types of thinking cheaper, large language models make yet other types of thinking cheaper. These breakthroughs are dots on a long line of progress of ever cheaper thinking, with the steady progress on the underlying hardware perhaps even more decisive than the progress on the software that gets much of the attention.

We should expect more such breakthroughs with progress in fields like quantum computing, perhaps also photonic computing. And we should include the progress in the two main inputs to cheap thinking as well: the generation of ever cheaper electricity through renewables or next generation forms of nuclear power and the generation of ever cheaper and ever more precise measurements and sensing of the environment through mobile networks and quantum sensing for instance.

Cheap thinking is the sum of technological breakthroughs and of applying theses as to shift how information is generated, processed and acted upon from humans to cheap machines. If we want to keep a catchy abbreviation, then we should perhaps move from AI for artificial intelligence to pAI for pervasive artificial intelligence - which is nice also because pAI sounds like pi or 3.14.

Of course, we need to proceed with caution as we move into predictions. Patterns and laws of the past need not hold in the future. Just put yourself into the shoes of poor Malthus who has been proven so thoroughly wrong. Back in his day, the past and the present seemed to show unequivocally and mathematically that the mass of people was condemned to living close to subsistence levels because of their desire for more children. Could he have foreseen the shift from agriculture to industry and with that the sustained and significant increase in living standards of commoners? I doubt it.

(1) Baseline predictions

Still, we need to venture into the future. And we start with four baseline developments that appear very clear to forecast.

(a) pAI systems will overtake individual humans in their performance of any cognitive task.

The question is not whether they surpass humans, the question is rather how far they will go beyond. Just keep in mind that the human brain is limited in its cognitive capacity by, among other things, its volume, which for most of us is somewhere between 1100 to 1300 cubic centimetres. That's quite a bit as far as animals of our size go, but it still imposes some very real trade-offs on our mental abilities in the complex environment of the modern world.

There is a physical limit to intelligence, and we shall revisit this point and its implications further below, but that limit is still very far out. Just think of the stories of gifted people with specific standout cognitive abilities, like present day savants and historical geniuses, they give you a taste of what is possible in terms of intelligence. In fact, imagine them and then give them not a lifetime of experience but the combined experience of millions of man-years. That's where we are eventually going.

A small taste of what is to come, and for me personally the eureka moment, was the release of AlphaGo back in 2016 and its sequence of games against one of the highest rated go players of the time, Lee Sedol. Having played against competing versions of itself millions and millions of times to train - as if Lee Sedol had played against twins of his for thousands of years - AlphaGo made moves that were incomprehensible to even the most seasoned go commentators. And some of these moves turned out to be crucial building blocks for winning the game. This was possibly the first time that we observed an intelligence at work whose thought processes are beyond our comprehension.

When thinking about the impact of pAI it is very tempting to compare pAI systems to individual humans. But that is just a small part of the equation. No human is intelligent and knowledgeable enough to send a rocket to the moon or to design and produce a smartphone. But groups of people, acting and thinking in coordination can. Groups of people acting in coordination are the highest-level intelligence that we know. The more interesting question therefore is what impact pAI will have on organisations. We will revisit this further below when we show how bureaucratic organisations are going to evolve into technocratic organisations through pAI.

(b) Value creation is going to continue going up.

The second very clear prediction we can make is that economic output is going to go way up. Thinking is a key input everywhere you look and it becoming cheaper will make us as society overall a lot more productive. This is true for topics as widely dispersed as entertainment, corporate planning, the judiciary, and health care.

If you combine cheap thinking or pAI with robotics you get into a world of abundance in yet another meaning of the word. Will this by itself resolve the majority of wants in the world? Clearly no. This type of abundance will give us new tools to address challenges like climate change, diseases, malnutrition and lack of education - giving us more options and lowering the costs of getting things done on these fronts. But at the same time it will not by necessity lead to a socialist utopia and global peace. And that is because the abundance will be rather unevenly distributed.

(c) Value creation is going to become yet more concentrated.

Since time immemorial some people were more productive than others. When stone age hunters went on their trips the more experienced hunters with better eyesight or hearing, with a steadier hand and a better feel for the spear bow were contributing more to the success of the hunt than the inexperienced, the short-sighted, the clumsy. They contributed more, but not dramatically more. Suppose the best hunter fell ill, the rest of the hunters could likely still be successful enough on the hunting trail to feed the tribe. And the clumsy and inexperienced youngsters were learning and improving so as not be a drag on the rest of the hunters for long.

As with other waves of technology before it, the pAI wave is going to accentuate the difference between the most productive and the least productive members of as society. Where a person used to be perhaps 50% more productive, they can now we 5 times more productive or 5 thousand times more productive.

Let's go through one small modern day example to illustrate. Finding a taxi and being driven around town to one's destination used to be very much the cognitive task of the local taxi driver. In London for instance, to become a cabbie required you to learn the maze of streets by heart and to be able to navigate yourself and the passengers through it. This was called, with high respect, 'the knowledge'. In fact, you needed more knowledge than a navigational understanding of London: you needed to build an understanding of when to go where to capture demand for trips; you also needed robust communication skills to understand what the tourists were saying, and you also needed a repertoire of recommendations. Then came pAI in the form of mobility apps that enabled customers to order a taxi remotely to wherever they happened to be, and to specify their destination in the comfort of their native language. The taxi driver did not need 'the knowledge' anymore, he was instructed where to turn left or right by the app, and he did not need to know how to communicate, how to do his pricing and his payments, none of it. All he needed to do was driving the car. And eventually of course, one would no longer need a human driver either. But let's stick to the taxi driver for a moment: his or her value contribution to the taxi drive was drastically cut down by the emergence of the app. To see this one needs to remind oneself that value that used to be delivered by 1000 taxi drivers was then delivered by 1000 taxi drivers and say 10 techies that build and maintain the mobility app. The distribution of value between these two groups is of course contentious and a question of bargaining. Yet the market outcomes are clear and strongly suggest that the techies contribute a very substantial share. And suppose now in a thought experiment we move from 1000 taxi drivers and 10 techies to 10 techies with robot taxis and no taxi drivers. We can then argue the following: the 1000 taxi drivers were taxi drivers because that was the highest productivity job they could find in the society, and their pay reflected that productivity. The 10 techies, their app and their 1000 robot taxis together bring the same value contribution as the 1000 taxi drivers did before. Then the average value contribution of a techie is 100 times the average value contribution of a taxi driver. If you now consider that in 2023 there were not 1000 taxi drivers in London but close to 20,000 and that the mobility apps do not only work in London but in many large cities, then you see that the productivity difference between the techies and the taxi drivers need not be limited to a factor of 100 times, it can easily go to 100,000 times.

One could of course try to make the counterargument that the world would still spin without the techies and their apps and that the value generation of the taxi drivers would still work, and hence the actual value contribution of the techies is low. In effect saying that the techies were just clever in how to grab the value contributions of the taxi drivers. This may be true to a degree, but it is also immaterial. The fact remains that the customers value the contribution of these techies and their ant-like drivers or their robot taxis the same as the classical taxi drivers beforehand. Whether fairly or not, the techies are being as productive as the taxi drivers used to be, and thus on individual basis something like 100,000 times more productive.

To put that into perspective, go back to our hunter gatherer friends. It is not easy to imagine a stone age hunter so proficient and gifted to be able to outweigh the work and contribution of more than a handful or a dozen of regular hunters working as a team. I would posit even that the tens of thousands of years of our hunter gatherer history across the globe have never witnessed a hunter that would be as effective and productive as 100,000 regular hunters. And yet that's what we just derived is the ratio for the mobility techies and the taxi drivers.

The example of the taxi drivers is salient because so many people will see and experience this change in their lifetime and in real life. Yet there are and will be countless other examples that happen out of sight. Take warehouses for instance. The workers in these used to know how to navigate the aisles, how to store and retrieve items in an efficient way. Today, even if not fully automated, the workers in these warehouses can better be thought of as biological robots that receive instructions of what to do not day by day but rather 10 seconds by 10 seconds.

Suppose you lined up 100 million working age adults around the turn of the millennium and ordered them by their value contribution as allocated by our market mechanisms; the highest productivity people to the left and then in descending order towards the right. The drop-off would be very steep initially and then flatten out for the bottom three quarters or two thirds. Think of a distribution akin to the 80/20 rule: something like 20% of people generate something like 80% of the value.

Now suppose you repeat this exercise in the year 2100, with pAI fully present and adopted. We would no longer look at a curve that resembles the 80/20 rule. We would be looking at a curve that resembles a 99/1 rule. Something like 1% of the people generate something like 99% of the value. And this may well be still a generous interpretation. What is behind this of course is not that the Techies in and of themselves are now superhuman, what is behind this is that they control the machines. And against that backdrop it is also clear that 'the techies' is a shorthand for the union of the actual techies, their capital backers and the builders of these machines.

(d) Large sections of knowledge get commoditised.

It is important in this context to be clear on what exact value generation is shifting. The big news in the examples above is not the lower demand for labour as in the labour that taxi drivers and warehouse workers used to supply. The big news there is the devaluation of local knowledge. Knowing the map of London like the palm of one's hand was the key knowledge asset that the taxi drivers leveraged and got paid for. This was local knowledge that the tourist for instance would not possess. Walking the aisles and being able to figure out how to best walk the aisles was also an important contributor to the productivity of a warehouse worker. All this knowledge is now centralised and available to the machine to work with – without having to rely on the local knowledge of the worker. This knowledge is commoditised and can cheaply be bought.

And local knowledge is actually just one example of what we could call tacit knowledge. Tacit knowledge is what you know without being able to articulate what you know. "Know it when I see it" would be an example. Or "at the end, season the dish to your liking". One commercially important example is doctors diagnosing illnesses based on their training and experience. This is their tacit knowledge and a key if not the central building block of their status and value creation. More and more such tacit knowledge is going to become explicit knowledge and with that the control over this knowledge is going to move either into the public domain or to whoever controls the key algorithms and systems of pAI.

(2) What does this mean for elite commoner relationships?

Let's start by going through the bargaining framework again that we introduced when discussing hunter gatherers.

Starting with the elite members or the leaders, it is clear that verifying the work of the commoner or follower will be cheaper and more precise. Sensing, monitoring and judging will be aided by machines, to large extent outsourced to machines. The discretionary area of work for many commoners is going to shrink. The only exception to this rule is the fraction of a percent of commoners that are the new superstar brainies that are required to design and run pAI systems, science programs, and manage business concerns as for instance corporate executives and entrepreneurs. Except for these special cases, directing and keeping in control of commoners is now easier for the elite.

Moving on to the commoners, the most damaging news for them is that retaliation against the elite is now much harder. With agriculture and manufacturing increasingly automated by smart robots, most commoners work in service jobs, which we saw above are worse in terms of enabling retaliation. How about ratcheting the pressure up and down when retaliating? Being able to fine-tune the pain is important but is also getting harder to do. It starts with elites being more mobile than before. They jet set around the globe, and their assets live in the electronic world based in data centres with layers of redundancy built in. And the services they consume and the systems through which they create value are more dispersed and global. Commoners in a certain locale are very substitutable, there is precious little in terms of ratcheting up or down that is noticeable. So it is pretty much either being compliant on the one hand and being in full swing rebellion on the other. And going into the latter has a rather high threshold for most people.

But it gets worse. Judging the merits of the leader is also harder. The world has always been a complex place, but it is possibly becoming even more so. Plus, understanding what is possible and what is fanciful used to be common sense exercise. With pAI and its abundance it is going to be harder to properly gauge what is affordable and what is not. And with substance more difficult to convey, appearances and propaganda will exert greater influence. Expect more political theatre and spin doctors.

Moving on to how to coordinate against leaders. This one is interesting because the low cost of communication helps people understand how others feel and helps them mobilise. But then it is obvious that the elite will move quickly to take control of the media and communication networks also in this new world. And the elites have the advantage. Just look at the Arab Spring earlier this century in which regimes of fairly low technological sophistication managed to take control over communication networks of the masses.

Finally, let's review how aligned the preferences are between the elite and commoners. The short answer is less than before, as we discussed in the services economy outlook above.

The perhaps hardest message, however, is that the old quasi-elites are going to be severely weakened if not made disappear: the lawyers, the doctors, the managers, the tax advisors. Of course there will still be doctors and lawyers, but doctors and lawyers being occupations for a very significant part of the population through which one can work itself into a quasi-elite status via a lifetime of dedication? That is going to disappear. The average doctor, the average lawyer, the average manager, all these people will cease to be relevant. They are the next level taxi drivers.

All this sounds like we are essentially going back to a power balance akin to agrarian times. The pharaoh and his high priests supported by the top talent in the form of scribes. Who in turn oversee the work of 98% of the population toiling in the fields, quarries and workshops.

Or is it? Will people still be needed in the fields, quarries and workshops?

(3) The question of employment

The good news is that there is nothing like a fixed amount of work to be done in a society.

If you feel a need for proof that new technological opportunities are not used to just make life continue as before but with more leisure, then you need to look no further than the share of the Amish people in the United States. At the time of writing, they comprise less than 0.2% of the total population - their lifestyle does not seem to attract lots of converts.

New technological opportunities from cheap thinking will likewise lead to new gimmicks, new experiences and so on, rather than just making things cheaper. And those things that do get cheaper, such as all kinds of entertainment and advice will see their consumption increase headily. When the cost of a good drops dramatically, then typically its demand goes up. This is known as the price elasticity of demand.

When demand picks up as costs drop, the number of people employed in the activity producing the good that the technological revolution touches may go up even as the labour input per unit decreases. If demand all in goes up sufficiently then total number of workers in an industry stays the same as cheap energy and cheap thinking make every single worker more productive and machines take over more and more tasks.

So far for the theory. Alas in real life, there are certain inherent limits on how much demand can go up. Most demands are not ultimately 'insatiable' as economists typically assume. And these demand limits come from physical limitations. Starting with our bodies, it is clear that we have certain limitations in our digestive capacity, in our athletic capacity and our sexual capacity – putting a ceiling on for instance the amount of food we demand. Few people

have a desire for more than a few bigger meals a day. And so it should not surprise us that the share of income going into buying food has been declining as incomes have risen.
There is also a time constraint in that a day has only 24 hours for everyone. All the entertainment, all the news and all the other content has at the very maximum 70 trillion hours a year to fill for a population of 8 billion humans. There is also a cognitive capacity constraint in terms of the complexity and amount of information to take in – this extends from user manuals of board games to storylines of novels.

Cheap energy and manufacturing were a very happy case when looked at through this lens: demand picked up dramatically, the natural limits on demand are also very far out – people have no problem with owning a new phone every year, along with a host of other gadgets, and the super-rich find space for dozens of cars in their homes. And while the Industrial Revolution has been lowering the labour intensity of manufactured goods, i.e. the work time of humans needed per final manufactured piece, it is still substantial. And so the demand for humans in manufacturing grew strongly as the Revolution spread, certainly over the first 1.5 to 2 centuries. Manufacturing employment may have plateaued or shrunk in developed countries, but it may actually still be gently growing internationally.

So, what is the verdict on cheap thinking going to be?

Cheap thinking will accelerate the decline in employment in agriculture and manufacturing. We talked about the limits of demand of food and we can see employment in agriculture plummeting over the centuries since the Industrial Revolution. Mechanisation is continuing this path with the help of pAI.

Manufacturing will eventually follow a similar path. Already in 1999, the then chairman of the Federal Reserve, Alan Greenspan, remarked that "the physical weight of our gross domestic product is evidently only modestly higher today than it was 50 or 100 years ago" - meaning more growth in demand happened outside of (heavy) physical goods. The limits of demand are further out than with food but we are starting to near saturation in some areas. And with limited upswings in demand further automation through pAI and robotics will reduce the number of jobs.

Services and experiences are thus the new frontier of employment. And here, AI will make many brainy sectors less labour intensive, but not only that. And as outlined above, the talent concentration is going to be much more pronounced than in agriculture and manufacturing: the value generation gap between the least productive 10% and the most productive 10% of workers goes from being measured in percentages to being measured in orders of magnitude. With near costless replicability and transferability this 'superstar effect' will only strengthen. And we have the time constraint of the 24 hours in a day kicking in. Entertainment, games, virtual reality, these are not going to be the employment drivers of the future.

Experiences in the real world is where employment may well go up strongly. These can be furnished better with the help of cheap energy and cheap thinking, but they still have a physical home, may depend on the physical setting as in tourism, and they build on human-to-human interactions for which we humans in all likelihood have a strong innate desire. We enjoy services being provided to us by other people. This signals a positive relative status and that is something we all seek. It also stands to reason that experiences are going to become the new status goods. The supply of many of them is inherently limited.

And so, while cheap thinking may well not bring about a surge in pleasurable work and employment opportunities for the great mass of people, it need not bring widespread unemployment either. We will have a surge in people helping provide experiences and services. People value the human interactions therein, and they will demand a lot more of these.

On top, human work in everything will be a status symbol to the person buying the good or service. Having your massage done by a perfect AI enabled robot may well be super cheap, basically free. Having a human masseur or masseuse on the other hand will cost a bit more. This is similar to the premium that antiques, artisanal crafts etc command today. This will grow big.

All this said, the value generated and, as we have argued above, the bargaining power of workers in these new employment opportunities will be lower than in manufacturing. While overall value generation and abundance in the economy grows, the share accruing to the masses will decrease.

Finally, we need to remember that elite members are of course concerned about their physical safety. In their own homelands at least, I expect it will in many cases be cheaper to provide fake jobs (or low impact jobs) to the masses rather than build a massive security apparatus to keep desperate, starving masses at bay. The unfortunate truth is that this logic would likely only apply to very circumscribed homelands. Keeping people in slum areas, as in erstwhile South African homelands not elite homelands, i.e. reservations at subsistence level has been a common occurrence in the 20th century. Expect apartheid make a comeback big time.

(4) What will happen to the masses?

We start with an admittedly extreme scenario.

The masses cease to be an economic asset. Instead, they are a 'breeding ground' for extreme talent, which then gets scouted and extracted to be co-opted to do actual work for the elite. The non-extreme talent, in other words the 99 point something percent of regular people are being appeased and sedated by a combination of social transfers, virtual reality games and parallel worlds as well as drugs.

Actual work will be done by machines and the extreme brainies and entertainers. Supported perhaps by an army of low-level service people, the 'worker ants'. Overall value generation will go up, but wages will fall.

This extreme scenario is certainly possible. And one can of course jump into a yet more extreme scenario by imagining the machines taking over from the elite and humans dying out. Ever since we started building nuclear bombs at scale in the 1950s humankind has held a finger at a trigger of wiping itself out. pAI is adding another trigger the elite is keeping a finger on. I wouldn't discount the odds of us pulling the trigger on one of these (and there may be more, such as new types of viruses bred in labs), whether by accident, whether by suicidal episode of a key decision-maker, or whether by emotional short circuit during escalating conflict between organisations.

That said, there is nothing inevitable in such possible paths to doom, and to navigate around these doom trigger points we had better understand our future societal setup, future organisational setup, and future preferences.

We thus go back to scenarios which still have humans in it. Next to the extreme one outlined above, the elite could also choose to drive towards a moderated one. In such a scenario, the share of income going to the masses will still decrease alright, but life as a member of the masses will nonetheless be good. There is no want of security, food, shelter, gadgets and entertainment; and if you so wish you can even advance your status and consumption a little bit compared to your peers by taking up service jobs and getting good at them. Cheap food, cheap energy, cheap thinking creates a materially comfortable life for everyone, and a life of unimaginable abundance and power for a small elite.

Whether societies end up in the extreme dystopian or the moderate scenario will depend mostly on the outlook and preferences of the future ruling elites - and on whether they have the coordination mechanisms to turn these preferences into action.

Looking back at the quote from the beginning of the chapter, what will the aggregate moral compass be of the elite? Will elites feel shame for running a badly governed country with crazy wealth existing side by side with destitution? Or will they want to and manage to take good care of those left behind?

A simple answer would be that there is no reason to believe that elites today are by disposition any more or any less selfish than elites 1000 years ago or 1000 years hence. By way of genetic disposition and by way of elite members, in climbing the social ladder, being selected for ruthlessness this is true. But that is not the full picture as individual preferences change with technology and wealth.

When you are at a subsistence level income, your thoughts and desires are naturally focused on making ends meet in the here and now. Thinking too much about the longer-term future, about abstract concepts like fairness and freedom is not on your mind – because it would be dangerous to have that on your mind. You need all your brainpower and will to survive.

With your nutrition, shelter and other more basic needs securely satisfied and taken care of long term, you can afford to direct your attention to topics that influence your emotional well-being less urgently. Social justice causes, environmental causes, the arts, these things then take up an expanding share of your thinking time.

And when people become financially free, so that they have full agency over their time, have the full barrage of tools of society at their disposal, and can get access to the decision-makers in society, their outlook changes yet again. They may start thinking about bringing about structural change to the world and leaving a lasting legacy.

The key question therefore becomes: are future elites going to feel sufficient kinship and altruism towards the masses to afford them a decent life; and will the societal setup enable them to coordinate to make that happen?

To have a chance at answering which of these scenarios, the dystopian or the moderate one, we will see emerge we need to understand how the elite is going to organise itself in the coming post-democratic society. Let's turn to that.

Chapter 5: A guide to what comes after democracy

"The Republic was in fact ruled as an aristocratic oligarchy by about 20 to 30 families of Venice's urban nobility, who elected the Doge of Venice, held political and military offices, and directly participated in the daily governing of the state. They were predominantly merchants, with their main source of income being trade with the East and other entrepreneurial activities, on which they became incredibly wealthy."
Wikipedia on the Venetian nobility, accessed in May 2024.

So, what does the preceding chapter mean for the setup and organisation of societies?

We have seen that the agrarian societies tended to be monarchies, almost exclusively so. We have also seen that manufacturing-based societies tended to be democracies, with the notable runner up alternative of meritocratic autocracies. pAI based societies will have a yet different stable equilibrium, or set thereof.

Before we dive in one thing to keep in mind:

The setup of a society is more like an organism, less like a designed machine. We should not necessarily think of the new organisational setup in the pAI world as a revolution with a wholesale new setup and elite. It may in most cases very well be an organic development where certain mechanisms and actors are strengthened while the power of other withers. Think of the United Kingdom which, in the wake of the Industrial Revolution, has retained many of the trappings of a monarchy while the monarch has in fact relinquished all decision-making power to the elected government. The societal setup has transitioned from monarchy to democracy without any hard cuts.

It should therefore not surprise us if different current societal setups evolve towards a similar actual decision-making and governance solution without shedding completely their traits as monarchies, democracies, theocracies, autocracies - or some new form we do not know yet. This we could call convergent evolution as in biology where, as an example, the eyes of vertebrae (like ours) and the eyes of arthropods (like those of insects) capture the same underlying opportunity afforded by physics - but from different starting points. To exploit the differences in intensity and angle of reflected sunlight for navigating one's environment, they both have developed lenses and light receptors, but they follow very different design principles with a single lens vs a multi-lens (or compound eye) approach.

Looking back it was the same thing with industrialisation: It required a setup that enabled high labour mobility, secure private property rights, high general taxation to pay for public transportation infrastructure and public schooling, while enabling the emerging industrialists a path to join the elite. This did not require democracy per se, it did not require autocracy either. But it was clearly at odds with the dynamics of feudal systems with serfdom. Eventually, for mature manufacturing societies with a large quasi-elite, democratic mechanisms were more conducive to coordinate the elite around the economic opportunities and outcompeted monarchies; and for the most part autocracies, too.

(1) From labour mobility to data mobility

There will be convergent evolution in the pAI world as well. And much like democracy solved the challenges of labour mobility to exploit the Industrial Revolution to the full, the societal creatures of this evolution will be the ones that solve the challenges to exploiting pAI to the full. More concretely:

The now emerging new elite members are data generation processes owners and algorithms owners. Their interests are different from old style industrialists. They don't need large workforces of well-educated workers; they just need a few exceptional ones. They also do not need public infrastructure that much. What this also means that the interests of these new elite members diverge more from the interests of the masses than the interests of the erstwhile industrialists. Among other things this means the appeal of democracy to the elite all in decreases. Or in other words, the cost of doing business through democracy stays high and the benefits for the average elite member are lower. The masses cannot be trusted to do the right thing, and they are not that important anymore either.

Data generation owners and algorithm owners dislike democracy. Instead, they go for technocrats. Those are armed with data, theories and algorithms, and are steered through the reporting of "key performance indicators" set by the elite. Plus they can be cost effectively monitored and controlled by yet another set of technocrats called academics. Central banks have led the way. Other areas will follow. All the while democratic actors are increasingly relegated to theatrical performances.

Genuine democracies will protect the vested interests of the decentral information processors who were pivotal in the manufacturing economy as 'quasi-elites': the lawyers, doctors, architects, tax advisors, civil servants, mid-level management, accountants etc. And because they protect them, they will not be the winning political system of the cheap thinking economy. These vested interests will need to be broken, and you will need strong central authority to overcome the local resistance. You also need deep pockets in the central authority to buy off the more important parts of them. Breaking these 'quasi-elites' is going to be one of the big questions of the 21st century. The political system that accomplishes this without triggering catastrophic civil war or its own dissolution will be the torchbearer system for the digital economy. Whatever system wins will need strong central authority and deep pockets.

While this is one of the big questions, the main challenge, the overriding question, the one that is as central as the labour mobility question for the Industrial Revolution, is the question of data mobility. The question of how to coordinate the elite to pool data and intelligence.

Like human intelligence, pAI is about gathering information, processing it, and thereby creating new information. You need infrastructure, algorithms as well as institutional and legal frameworks – but what is clearly different from before, what is not easily solved with the legacy tools of the manufacturing age, is how to enable, incentivise and coordinate the sensors and their data flows between sensors and computing and decision-making nodes.

The societal setup that better controls and coordinates the flow of data and information will win. What good are algorithms on their own after all. Besides, they are easy in principle to be copied and to be diffused. Just a little bit of information after all. Just think of Sherlock Holmes who would not solve his cases without data: "It is a capital mistake to theorise before one has data".

The established quasi-elite will aim to slow down data mobility, after all their principal asset is the knowledge and judgement they have acquired through training and experience - in other words a data set they carry around in their heads. Unfortunately for them much of this data is relatively straightforward to capture in machine readable form and at scale. Other knowledge and judgement heavy jobs will be more difficult to have machines learn it because there is no collected data. Think of most managerial and political positions and roles. But this, too, will only be a transitory state.

Data generation may well be a good yardstick of the cheap thinking revolution; and it has exploded in recent decades. And yet, data generation today is nothing compared to what it could be and will be. To put that into perspective consider the trajectory of energy use, one of the yardsticks of the cheap energy revolution.

Imagine you surveyed global energy use on the eve of the First World War: as an unbiased observer you'd think that mankind was harnessing energy at a level totally different from whatever there was before the cheap energy revolution (the Industrial Revolution). And you'd be right, humankind was leveraging about three times as much energy compared to a hundred years before - and it was all very obvious in the developed world with factory smoke, railways everywhere, steamers on the oceans and electric lighting in the streets at night.

And yet you hadn't seen anything yet really. Another hundred years later, energy consumption has soared another ten times and the use cases where we leverage non-muscle energy have become ubiquitous. And what 1914 was to energy use, 2024 is to data generation.

So, what kind of societal setup are we going to converge to in the era of cheap thinking and data mobility?

Whatever the setup, it has to enable high levels of investment into sensors and data and computing centres. Even a benevolent setup will have to be what many people today would call a 'surveillance state' setup. We are moving into a translucent society, back to the roots in the sense that our forebears in both hunter gatherer and agrarian times did not know anonymity either.

And whatever the setup, it has to enable low friction movement of data between economic actors. Today we largely have vertically integrated companies that collect proprietary data, complemented with some publicly available data. In the future, societies that facilitate data pooling and cross-pollination between companies and other actors will outcompete those that stick to the current model.

And with local and devolved knowledge and data becoming more easily capturable and thus explicit, taken out of the monopoly of local decision-makers, there is going to be a trend towards greater centralization of decision-making.

So again, where does this take us? There are two extremes to be considered. One extreme is a mercantilist coalition of corporate and capital markets leaders, which if anything reminds me of the setup of the ancient Venetian Republic, "La Serenissima"; while the other extreme is a return to a largely centrally planned society and economy, which of course reminds one of the Soviet Union's state planning committee, the "Gosplan" (but as we will see there is a better, newer blueprint available that leans in on competition). I don't think the future will look like a Goldilocks middle ground between these two extremes, but before we get to discuss that we had better understand the two extremes.

(2) La Serenissima

Let's start with a somewhat more structured approach as to why we may end up with what we shall call the 'Venice Model' as the new dominant societal setup.

Organisations are coordination mechanisms. Firstly at the very top, and then in nested fashion cascading down. As coordination mechanisms they need to answer, among other things, these three key design questions:

(a) how much centralisation of decision-making to set versus decentral decision-making (the scope of the central roles if you will);

(b) how to pick the people to fill the top roles and to do the actual decision-making (the most pronounced issue being the succession problem); and finally
(c) what guardrails to put in place on their decision-making (this used to be all about religion, today this is also very much about constitutions, the checks and balances, and about public opinion).

Looking at centralisation, there are benefits of course to higher levels of centralisation: in the form of being able to leverage societal resources at scale, for instance in infrastructure investment for public use or in education and scientific research. In short, centralisation enables societies to invest where individuals or smaller coalitions struggle to make the investment cases because they cannot capture the benefits well. The cost of centralisation are lower incentives and motivation at the local level, as well as difficulties in creating the right understanding of what is happening on the ground, local and dispersed, and making the right decisions.

Agriculture based monarchies typically had low levels of centralisation, with either feudal lords or provincial bureaucrats enjoying very high degrees of autonomy of decision-making. Tellingly, bureaucratic centralisation was more successful where there were high societal gains to be had from collective action, as in the irrigation-based agriculture of the ancient Fertile Crescent for instance.

Manufacturing brought much higher levels of centralisation. The returns on public investment into infrastructure, education, colonies (whether explicit or implicit) and warfarin capabilities were high - and the costs became lower with improvements in communication technologies.

pAI based societies will see yet higher levels of centralisation. The returns on collective action remain high while the costs will be markedly lower. This of course means that the leading roles and positions of society are going to be yet more influential, and therefore the process for picking the leaders yet more momentous.

Which bring us to the question of succession. Civil wars are bloody and costly affairs. Societal setups that are better at avoiding them tend to outcompete similar ones that are prone to descending into them. And moments of succession of key positions of power are the neuralgic points where civil war can be sparked. Which is why the logic of choosing the successor typically mirrors the logic of who would likely emerge as the winner in a civil war.

In agrarian societies, the base of power was the allegiance of peasants on productive land. Their taxes fed and financed the armies with which to win a potential civil war. Now take feudal monarchies as an example: Where the king was the biggest landlord and bequeathed all his land to just one of his children, he could thus ensure that his chosen successor would likely prevail in a potential civil war - and thereby likely avoid a challenge to his chosen successor and a civil war altogether.

Viewed through this lens, elections in modern democracies are not so much about democratic legitimacy and not so much about serving the electorate, they are a mechanism for the elite to coordinate on decision-makers in a manner that avoids a civil war. As we discussed above, in manufacturing-based societies, the incentives between elite and populace are fairly strongly aligned - and hence the popular vote is a good indicator of who would win a civil war.

In a pAI based society, a very large part of wealth and power, and hence resources in the case of a civil war, come from corporate activities whose incentives are not well aligned with the general population. The popular vote will thus cease to be a good indicator which elite members would prevail. We can look at parallels in history get an inkling of what alternative mechanisms the elite might use:

pAI generates value and wealth not through producing things by working the land, not through producing things in factories, not through providing virtual experiences. It produces value through influencing people to do things the owners of the AI want them to do and by being the gatekeepers of what people get so see, learn, compare. If we look at the new elites rising on data generation processes and algorithms today, then we are looking at corporates that today work mostly on digital media, digital commerce and the digital devices that enable all these applications. Their outlook is inherently global in scope, and they tend to build their technological process flows and assets in a vertically integrated manner, i.e. with a high degree of central control. At the same time, their integration with humans tends to be through platforms, i.e. transactional, not relational – except the few superstar employees that work on the core mechanisms.

From the point of view of a person chosen randomly from across the globe, they closely resemble the world-faring merchants of pre-industrial times. They also hailed from faraway lands, arrived with mysterious and treasured wares as well as novel stories and views of the world. They were outside of your community, and often outside of your community's jurisdiction. In other words, they were similarly removed from the day-to-day lives of the people they transacted with, they similarly thrived on knowledge and daring, they similarly controlled the commercial choices of people, and similarly they aimed to influence and entice their commercial counterparts.

There have been a number of pre-industrial states and organisations that thrived on long distance commerce, some we encountered above. My favourite example in the present context is the merchant republic of Venice, also known as 'La Serenissima'.

In merchant republics like La Serenissima, with fortunes and thus relative strengths between families and individuals more shifting and volatile year after year, compared to the landed aristocrats, it was not so easy to build a dominant position and monopolise power. It could be done in principle, as the Medici did for a while in Florence or as Pericles did through personal charisma in ancient Athens, but these are exceptions to the rule. While agrarian society tended towards a stable and all-powerful ruler or monarch, trade-based societies tended towards oligarchies with shifting factions or coalitions controlling the succession process.

And so, one of the two extremes that I see we can plausibly end up in as dominant new state organisational setup is the Venice Model, a plutocratic oligarchy. And in keeping with the last section, after having been led by master hunters, kings and presidents, mankind in the future may well be led by new incarnations of 'doges'.

Let us also consider the guardrails that are going to be put in place on the power of the 'doge'. It is worth noting how strong a role, and throughout history, religion has played in restraining the choices that the leader of the elite could take. As a somewhat eclectic example, consider the instructions that Stephen I of Hungary, the first king and founder of Hungary, left to his son and intended successor Emeric. Of the roughly 2500 words about 500 are introduction and about half of the remaining 2000 ask his son to uphold Christianity and the church. In modern democracies, this is complemented or replaced by civic religion, such as belief in human rights.

The Republic of Venice is understood to have been more tolerant and less dogmatic in religious matters than its agrarian and monarchic contemporary societies. And one may therefore expect future pAI societies to likewise put lower emphasis on guardrails through religion. But interestingly, this need not be so. The higher centralisation, and hence the stronger power, of key decision-makers will make elite members potentially lean towards enacting more guardrails. And second, with higher levels of intelligence, decision-making may well become opaquer, and hence, again, the incentive to put guardrails on it may well increase.

(3) The Hefei model

There is an alternative to the Venice Model future. It is the future that develops out of a strong central state.

Markets in the Venice Model will be a lot more monopolistic, with greater market power concentrated in companies controlled by the elite Merchants. Apart from that markets and their price discovery mechanisms will function much like a century earlier. The actors will be better enabled thanks to pAI. But you see, to call financial markets more advanced and better at directing savings because of high frequency trading and machine learning based quant hedge funds is off on many levels. The workings of central states and government authorities on the other hand will more fundamentally benefit from pAI.

In the mid-20th century, the Soviet Union, among other states, implemented a state led economy based on central planning, the agency responsible for devising the plan being colloquially known as the 'Gosplan'.

Now, Gosplan was not particularly successful: it did not achieve the catch-up growth with the US-led West that Khrushchev dreamt about and articulated to the populace and foreign dignitaries. It led to misallocation of resources, waste, muted and warped incentives, environmental damage at a grand scale etc. The system was quietly shelved as in the Hungarian goulash communism with institutionalised 'look away policies'; or shelved with more fanfare as when Gorbachev called for the Perestroika, and its equivalent in China was shelved when Deng Xiaoping toured the South and declared any cat that catches mice is good whatever its colour.

Would a novel Gosplan with mid-21st century technology fare better? Many of the challenges that Gosplan struggled with would be more easily solvable: local information will be a lot more explicit and collectable by central authorities; quality definition and control is a lot more advanced; planning and operations research will have advanced by a century of scholarship.

More importantly, with the experience of China there will be a case study of how to marry central direction setting and a strong role of the state with entrepreneurial incentives and competition via free markets. The latter was popularised by the Economist in August 2023 as the "Hefei model": investment and enablement of selected industries by a local or provincial government with deep pockets, a venture capital and private capital arm, and a lot of discretionary decision-making power, pursuit of economic opportunities through private enterprise with high powered incentives. Fierce competition with the outside world, i.e. other localities and provinces in China, and of course global markets, coupled with cooperation within the local cluster, e.g. across steps of the value chain. Note that this approach can of course be nested, with local municipalities clustering and differentiating in focus within larger structures like provinces, and all the way up to the full nation state. And note that in the context of this discussion we should look at the 'Hefei Model' not as the final state but rather as the prototype state of its kind.

How would such a Hefei Model scenario solve the data mobility question? Compared to a classical free market approach the local or provincial authorities can nudge or mandate a higher level of data interoperability and sharing, and similarly can the higher-level authorities in the nested structure. This need not come at the expense of the work that industry bodies do in terms of norming and standardisation or that voluntary data exchanges and company collaborations do in terms of enabling data mobility between actors. But with a very high vested business interest, the authorities will be incentivised to step in whenever these mechanisms appear to be insufficient or overly slow. Data mobility would be dictated from the top, not reached by consensus in the Venice Model halls and chambers.

We mentioned above that breaking the quasi-elites of today's knowledge workers of lawyers, doctors and the like without triggering civil war will be a key challenge for enabling data mobility. Here, too, the Hefei Model compares favourably with manufacturing-era genuine democracies: Elite careers in the authorities is linked to economic performance of their area and that performance is linked to data mobility more than to the well-being of these quasi-elites. There are no votes to give more weight to their concerns and demands for protection from algorithms.

To make the last piece a bit more concrete with an example: where in the past teachers' unions lobbied against performance evaluations of teachers to protect the weaker members and to pre-empt evaluation pressure building for all their members, in the future doctors' unions will lobby hard not only against AI and robot technologies in the healthcare system, they will in all likelihood also lobby hard against collecting patient data on diagnosis, treatment and health outcomes. This sounds counterintuitive because it is clearly against the interests of patients, but it seems logical to me because with the feedback loop thus severed it will be much harder for pAI to learn how to diagnose and treat diseases and improve population health outcomes in general.

The Hefei Model future is an outlier scenario. Elites will struggle to coordinate to reach it because every single elite member would need to give up a lot of power compared to the baseline (or default) scenario of the Venice Model. For one elite member or one company to monopolise power for practical purposes would be very difficult because all other elite members and companies would have an overwhelming incentive to band together and preserve the Venice Model setup. Such takeovers did happen in agrarian republics, see the case of the late Roman Republic first taken over by a sequence of small elite coalitions called triumvirates and then eventually by the Principate, i.e. a single person. Reverse takeovers also happened in agrarian times as when the German emperors of the High Middle Ages ceded ever more powers to the club of aristocrats called the prince-electors.

While we therefore should not rule out transitions altogether, they appear more like exceptions than the norm. There may also be another exception in the form of a company or state department becoming the dominant or monopolistic power in a vassal state of the Venice Model - comparable to the way the East India Company of the United Kingdom amassed dictatorial power in much of India a few centuries ago.

The most plausible way to the Hefei Model future is one in which a society with a state that is already strong and exercises a high degree of central control masters pAI technologies - and in so doing does not allow the pAI entrepreneurs to accumulate wealth and power that would upset the starting balance of power between the central and state authorities and top wealthy elite members.

Among the bigger powers, I see only one serious contender for this top-down scenario today, and that is China.

(4) Cheap thinking and geopolitics

I can see both the Serenissima and the Hefei ways of enabling high data mobility work. And it is tempting to throw in the towel and declare that both have their pros and cons and that there is no more to be said about the future. Except to reference Machiavelli and say that, like in agrarian times, the feudal Venice Model system will be the more flexible, adaptable and durable vs the bureaucratic Hefei Model system being more efficient yet also brittle. But we can actually go a few steps further.

Bureaucratic societies can, in principle, be more efficient and can operate at larger scale than feudal societies - if competently managed that is. It is therefore tempting to conclude that the Hefei Model states, if they emerge at all (and we have seen they are less likely to be formed in the first place), will have the advantage over the Venice Model states. But there are two key dimensions where they have a disadvantage:

Number one is welcoming new people to the elite, and providing both new and old elite members with a secure, long term elite lifestyle. Monopolistic state power means every elite member and their assets are potentially at risk when their interests collide with the interests of the state. The secret weapon of Serenissima societies is thus going to be the ability to attract extreme entrepreneurs of the likes of present-day Elon Musk (and offering club membership to them), and the ability to offer eye-wateringly attractive packages to the broader set of extraordinary global talent. You don't need a highly trained or even large workforce. You need to be the focal point where the top 0.01% of global talent comes together. You need a great narrative, control over global media, great amenities for the rich at home, and you need a currency that everyone accepts and wants. Ideally the global reserve currency, a large chunk of landmass with desirable climate and vegetation. And you need good infrastructure for the rich, including financial services, health services, high end transport, security, and private education for their kids. If a Venice Model state can provide all of this and if this extreme global talent buys into its narrative of the Republic winning the future, they will be at a distinct advantage of attracting this extreme talent.

We can thus perhaps boil down the question to how crucial the work of a few tens of thousands globally sourced superstar talents is vs the work of a few million locally sourced talent is. And to the question of where the starting position is.

America is the prime society moving towards a Venice Model setup, and most network effects favour it as the incumbent. It is little wonder therefore that the rich of the world, the elite in short, are, at the time of writing, voting for America to win the 21st century. We can clearly see this in the capital markets.

I personally would be careful to vote like that. And here's why: It's very easy to get carried away by the new opportunities of pAI. If you monopolise entertainment or philosophy then that's great, but it doesn't enable you to coerce the world to do your bidding. You would need a near monopoly on technological ingenuity and thinking. If you controlled 80 or 90% of the world's thinking capacity on technology then yes, your economic and military might that follows from that will make you so strong that most other organisations will fall in line with you and cooperate with you rather than risking your wrath. But the minimum threshold on the share of thinking is very high. The perhaps unique time in our history thus far where this threshold was surpassed was the later 19th century when imperialist European countries, including their settler colony offshoots, commandeered the world.

And to properly leverage your new cheap thinking agents on technology you need to be in control of your environment, you need to be able to control your full supply chain. If you depend on other societies for your food, that's a key weakness. If you depend on other societies for your energy, that's a key weakness. If you depend on other countries for your manufacturing, that's a key weakness. Smart elites are not greedy and understand that they had better optimise for a mix, not just for the high end new pAI systems. Hefei Model societies will be less greedy and more balanced than Venice Model societies.

And then Hefei Model states may also figure out a way to draw in and incentivise a good proportion of the exceptional global talent. While at the time of writing this is not really on the horizon, the main Hefei Model contender, China, certainly has the ability to accomplish this. There are precedents in its history, as in the form of the Tang dynasty. And they could also draw on the experience of designated special economic areas from the late 20th century, with the island of Hainan being an obvious candidate.

Wait a second, you may now think, what about dimension number two? Well the story is similar here.

Number two is about making catastrophic top-down decisions. Venice Model states, like all decentralised states in general, endure more chaos and are less efficient and less effective, but they are more robust in the sense that their response to changes in the environment inevitably includes a bit of experimentation – and so approaches that work out well fast enough get noticed and copied by other decentral actors.

Five hundred years ago, Ming dynasty China took one such fateful misguided top-down decision when it shut down Zheng He's treasure fleet and effectively banned all ocean-faring vessels – thereby enabling the take-over of the South-East Asian trading system by the Portuguese and Dutch, and other Europeans later on, and thereby laying the foundations as well for the century of humiliation three hundred years later.

There is one clear way for Hefei Model states to avoid at least most of the pitfalls of these strategic mistakes: by focusing top-down decision making on foundational and infrastructure investments while leveraging experimentation through policy experiments (as in for instance free trade zones and similar) and through the competition between private enterprises. This copies the key elements of robustness from the Venice Model. And as an aside, dear reader, whenever you can afford it, you better choose more robustness over more efficiency.

In the end, no matter who will win the geopolitical contest, the Venice Model or the Hefei Model states, one popular question here is whether pAI (or just AI in this question) will become our new overlords or even exterminate humanity. While such scenarios can very clearly not be ruled out, it is futile to worry and to try to stop AI from progressing. Imagine you were the chief of a native American tribe and you were opposed to railroads and European technology coming into your lands on the grounds of the long-term climate change impact and the demoralising and dehumanising effects of large-scale media and social media. You would have been prophetic people today might say, but you would have also been swept away by the European settlers. You cannot stop technology, you can only ride and manage it.

What gives me hope is that elites have a very good track record in leveraging experts of much higher intelligence and erudition than their own - without handing over their sources of power. As long as the elite leverages AI the way they leverage savant knowledge workers today, and as long as the elite values the future wellbeing of their descendants, humans will have a future. The real danger lies in elite members competing for power and designing AI to help them boot out other elite members without constraints. This would be a political AI and it would be programmed to grab and hold on to power no matter what. When its master dies without obvious heirs things could go wrong. This is naturally a greater risk in the Venice Model scenario, so for humanity the Hefei Model scenario gives higher odds of survival.

So, are we now in a position to answer the question of whether we are going to end up in a dystopian or moderate scenario in terms of the outcomes for the commoners like us? We are getting closer, but I'm afraid we need to understand first the role of the consiglieri in the Venice Model and Hefei Model states as well as our future value systems. Let's turn to that now.

Chapter 6: A deep dive on the translucent society

"Big Brother is watching you."
George Orwell, 1949

High data mobility leads us to the translucent society in which organisations are structured and run with the help of AI consiglieres and in which the society level flow of data is enabled by large scale public infrastructure. Let's start with the infrastructure:

(1) Society level data mobility

Where in the past canals, ports, railroads, highways, airports, electricity transmission lines supplied the basic building blocks of infrastructure to a region, in the future we are going to be talking also about data infrastructure.

Our preview of this infrastructure starts with the very strange observation that in the West today investments into data are largely private in nature.

This used to be different. The governments of old compiled nautical tables and exact maps of their territories to enable their merchants a safe passage and precise calculations; thereby reducing uncertainty and costs. Later, governments established statistical offices to collect and publish census data; and as measures such as Gross Domestic Product and inflation were developed. Or look at land registries: these are maintained in virtually all developed countries as a public good helping the citizenry to keep track of who owns what and even enabling financial engineering through keeping track of mortgage entries on this land database.

This is good economics as data is non-rivalrous: one person using data in his or her decision-making does not affect the ability of the next person to also use the same piece of data. Unlike pieces of cake, pieces of data can be eaten many times by many decision-making algorithms. Seeing the cost of data generation, activation and distribution plummet, one would thus expect a surge of public investment, yet the opposite has happened – a near complete crowding out of public data infrastructure investments by private companies. One may cheer at this in the sense that the taxpayer is spared an expense but one should not forget a serious drawback to this state of affairs: data generation and usage is siloed in these companies. Their data wells are providing a club good in economic parlance. Next consider how very few people work for these companies: As of 2023, Google employed 98'000 people and Facebook 45'000. Add in Apple's 137'000 and Microsoft's 148'000 and you arrive at 0.6% of all employees in the United States having access to work with the data these companies generate. And with so few people working with potentially full access to these data silos it is clear that a large part of the potential is untapped or wasted (if not most of it). Ironically, Eric Schmidt, then CEO of Google, even quoted Bill Joy in a book of his saying 'most of the smartest people work for somebody else'.

There is a potential halfway analogue here with investments into transportation infrastructure in the 19th and 20th century: The early booms of canals and railroads were largely driven by private enterprises while the push for airports and highways were largely state-led. If anything, the case for society level investments and near universal access is stronger with data than with transportation.

Successfully adapting societies will arrive at mechanisms akin to patents and other intellectual property rights for data generation: rewarding and incentivising the data generator for their efforts while limiting the rights of exclusion and bringing data into the public domain eventually. Some critical pieces will follow fair use rules and mandatory licencing regimes. And in areas where data supply is too low from a societal point of view the state can jump in as 'data buyer of last resort' or 'data generator of last resort'.

Any cursory comparison of the natural and the social sciences will show an alarming data paucity in the latter compared to the former. No wonder we are discussing things like superconductivity and gene drives in one area and gender studies and the limits of Keynesianism in the other.

Imagine that society tracks consumption behaviour, exercise behaviour, work patterns, relationships, and medical records, enriched with other personal data like genome, education test scores, nutrition, parenting approaches, tax records, police records etc. Where we must peer through the fog as best we can today, we would be looking at a book that lies open on the desk. We would come to understand how the lives of individuals work in detail, and we would learn how to design interventions for societal benefit.

But wait a second, you may say, dear reader, is this not painting an Orwellian dystopia? There are two answers to this. The first is that data privacy, and the ability to live one's life in a sort of anonymous manner, is a historical curiosity. It is a byproduct of urbanisation and the swelling of cities following the Industrial Revolution. The vast majority of our ancestors lived either as a hunter gatherer or as a peasant, and either way within close-knit communities where members knew each other personally and where gossip was travelling faster than news on the Internet today. And the vast majority of our descendants will live in societies where data mobility recreates this small world even in the face of millions and billions of people living interconnected lives. It's just a fact of life, like the passing on from democracy.

The second answer is that we think of privacy mechanisms in a somewhat primitive way today. We enforce it largely through restrictions on the collection of data. 'Nip it in the bud' if you like. This blunt approach makes sense in a world in which a society loses little by not collecting and using personally identifiable data while the individual may suffer grave harm from inappropriate or malicious use of their data. It is a bad deal for society overall if the considered use of such data unlocks great opportunities. And we certainly live in the latter world.

While our descendants will look back on the anonymity of the big city as an interesting episode in history, we also have to also acknowledge that some data is simply sensitive in nature. And the more data you put together and connect in relationships, the more sensitive it becomes in terms of yielding insights that can be leveraged to great effect for good and for evil. Many readers will think of this in terms of privacy, but it equally has military, political, commercial, terrorism, and other dimensions as well. Sensitivity has an element of what type of data you are handling, what granularity the data has, what interconnectedness (contextualisation), and also what latency (how old it is).

This is where trusted data calculation centres will come into play. These will function as collectors of data in the manner of a black hole: lots going in, nothing coming out. Third parties can work on and analyse this data, perform calculations, train and evaluate algorithms, configure reports, statistics and alerts and so on – but not access individual pieces of data or data sets. They only get the answers to their calculations which are checked to be aggregates conforming to a policy. The police and secret service will of course be very interested to learn what kind of requests people submit... And there will of course be use cases and actors that have higher levels of clearance and access.

New algorithms do not only need data. They also need to be tested. Imagine you are in charge of identifying and stopping criminals who try to defraud your digital payment service. A possibly surprising element of this work is that you will let some of the identified fraudster through the defences on purpose – so as to test whether your algorithms are correctly identifying fraudsters or whether the share of good customers inadvertently falling foul of your logic (the so-called 'false positives') is too high. You will need similar mechanisms at a societal level, too. It is not just the free trade zones, even though they are important testing grounds, this is a general attitude change that we will learn for how we bring new technology to life and enable it to learn and become mature.

Whenever societies in the past realised the enormous societal benefits of massed investment and broad access to new types of infrastructure, successful societies eventually marshalled the resources for public provisioning. Think canals and railroads in the 19th century, highways and public education in the 20th century. In the 21st century, successful societies will be investing multiple percentage points of their GDP into data infrastructure.

An unafraid society will turn itself into a translucent society; it will capitalise on the falling cost of data generation across a host of areas including controversial and feared areas such as facial recognition, genetic fingerprinting, and merging of health and public administration data with social interaction data – and making it accessible through trusted data calculation centres to anyone willing to pay for the incremental computational costs.

As an aside, a corollary or side effect of the translucent society is that there will be essentially no crime that involves physical violence. Law enforcement will have such overwhelming advantages over potential criminals that only the most passionate and irrational violent crimes occur.

Ancient cities typically had city walls. Ancient Rome, at the height of its power, lacked one for a couple of centuries. It must have looked bewildering to the first-time visitor from the provinces or abroad. But so great was the dominance of Rome's empire that there was no need to protect the city itself. And we will have similar action in inaction when it comes to personal protection in the translucent society.

There is a qualitative difference between a very low probability of certain adverse events and a zero probability of certain adverse events. We know that people care about the difference a lot because they pay very large amounts of money to rid themselves of such small probabilities. And we know these amounts by the name of insurance premiums.

Having some risks go down to essentially zero will free up a lot of brain space and resources for other endeavours. Generally speaking it will simply take out a layer of complexity from a vast class of problems.

(2) The AI consigliere and the rise of the technocratic organisation

Every organisation, be it a startup or a corporation, a church or a state, requires mechanisms for its members to be directed, coordinated and motivated. And these mechanisms we can think of as information processing machines which – in the form of headquarters, administrations, or governments – sit on top of processes that produce the actual products and services that sustain them. Their information processing works through many brains, plus paper and pens, plus computers – and increasingly plus pAI.

It is not news for humans to employ specialist experts that know a lot more about their expert domain and are potentially also much smarter than their managers. It is also not news that organisations leverage information processing machines. After all, one of our earliest forms of writing (and abstract mathematics) was possibly developed initially with the sole purpose of enabling the bureaucrats of Ancient Mesopotamia to do better accounting and bookkeeping. And today organisations employ digital accounting systems of vast proportions, and have complemented this with algorithms of cunning smartness. All of this has made organisations more effective, efficient, and also larger.

There is another step-change in smartness coming, as pAI will be employed not only as an expert down in the ranks, like today, but as a 'consigliere' up at the top of the decision-making hierarchy.

I take the term 'consigliere' from the leadership structure of the mafia as popularized in the 'The Godfather' series that follows an Italian-American mafia family through generations, and in which the bosses of the familia employ what they call a consigliere: a right-hand man and advisor, often highly competent in legal and administrative domains, and considered trustworthy through a symbiotic relationship with the boss cultivated over a long stretch of time, preferably starting in childhood. And what Tom Hagen was to Michael Corleone, pAI assistants or AI consiglieri are going to be to the bosses in the future.

To see how these will lead to dramatic improvements, we just need to follow the steps that information is worked through between people working in organisations. We start with passing information up the chain of control.

Whether we are looking at a mafia boss who needs to understand what is happening to his soldiers in the street, where business opportunities are developing and where rivals are working to grab territory; whether it is a politician asking much the same questions for his or her country; whether it is corporal or general in an army or an executive in a corporation – information has to be gathered about the environment and the inner workings of the organization, and then condensed and passed up the reporting lines. We talked about Ancient Mesopotamia's cuneiform early accounting as a way to make this process more effective, and today's digital technologies make such measurement and accounting exercises of course much easier. But then many of the larger, strategic questions are not answerable by way of counting events and commodities. They rely on more abstract interpretations of the world, and the counterfactual scenarios of the future when one's own moves are eliciting responses from other actors in the world.

This is where the AI consigliere will play a big role. Aggregating and selecting information to pass on and up the chain of command between human actors today is fraught with issues: from wanting to look good and filtering out bad news (or, conversely, from painting and overly dark picture to drum up support or as an excuse for one's failings), to not connecting the dots (i.e. not seeing the bigger picture and thus filtering out vital details for want of recognising their importance), and on to the very general issue of compressing information being a difficult task in any case (and some humans being better at this than others). No wonder that we have expressions like "the unfiltered truth from the frontline" and no wonder we talk about government officials and corporate executives as being "far removed from reality".

So, how does the consigliere help? By being the eyes and the ears of the boss, the fly on the wall and the satellite in the sky – and by being able to succinctly distil all that it perceives into a narrative of relevant information, into a version of the truth.

This will work off the fact that, compared to a single human, an AI has a much higher potential bandwidth, to use a technical term, of consuming information, taking in reams of data, conversations, pictures and what not. There is no need to compress information in multiple steps across a sequence of brains who are, mark the language we customarily use, 'one reporting (in)to the other' – with all the errors that accrue over the steps. Rather, the AI would do this in one swell swoop, as if it was as one big brain processing and compressing the information. And the AI can do this without the incentive misalignment issues (or with less of these issues at least).

Let's make this more concrete with an example. Suppose we wanted to know how the population of a country perceives the pros and cons (or the strengths and weaknesses) of their politicians of the day, their parties, and their policies and manifestos, along with the state of their nation and their hopes and concerns. In the absence of AI we have two avenues of getting a sense of what is on people's mind. One is to devise a highly structured questionnaire and conduct a poll or a census, then aggregate the responses by way of counting (which can be parallelised into say thousands of voting stations, without endangering the integrity and consistency of the results). The other avenue is to collect impressions and feedback in a less structured way in the form of individual interviews – or what the industry calls 'focus groups'. This gives rise to a much richer understanding of individual voices of course. These interviews are grouped into buckets which can then each be summarised by an individual (who would also be looking for similarities and other patterns as well as interesting outliers). And these summaries would be again grouped and summarised, with the process repeating until one human brain can ingest and comprehend all the summarised information with acceptable effort and time expended. An AI system can combine the advantages of both of these methods by being able to ingest and comprehend much larger chunks of information. Fewer parallelised summaries mean fewer connections and patterns between groups are lost. And it also means that the full population insights can be brought to life with details from archetypical individual views with a much higher level of confidence and validity.

In short, whether in this example or others, the AI consigliere will furnish the boss not only with a much broader and more reliable summary of what is happening but also furnish him with a lot more depths of understanding. Take a moment to consider what a change this will mean for the cosy world of the quasi-elite knowledge workers of today, the middle managers, the lawyers, the doctors: they will no longer be the ones who summarise and rationalise what is happening, there is this consigliere who has seen and knows as much or more as them. Welcome to the translucent society.

What are the implications? Well, flatter hierarchies for one. You don't need that much middle management anymore to aggregate and process information and to keep the soldiers in check. All you need is a few very senior people paired up with their respective consiglieri.

We already see this happening where commerce is shifting to digital marketplaces. Where in the old days, the marketing, trading and supply chains would have been organised through large bureaucratic hierarchies (think department stores), in the new digital world these hierarchies of middle management do not exist. Instead, we have people and companies connected to and steered on behalf of the marketplace by algorithms. And marketplaces are so simple that you do not even need AI for this steering.

And we also already see the potentially dark side of this: the consiglieri are going to be immensely influential. They are going to be the ones constructing the commercial and organisational truth on which much decision-making will rest.

Second, we move on to the complexity level of the mental frameworks. If conceptual information processing is done by humans, then naturally their mental frameworks are exerting a certain limiting pressure on the complexity and appropriateness of the emerging overall mental models that the organisation seems to make its decisions with.

When thinking quantitatively, humans tend to fall back on proportional, or linear, relationships between entities. If it takes three eggs to bake one cake, then I will need six eggs to bake two cakes. Alas, many relationships between entities in the real world are non-linear. My primary school math teacher in one of our lessons asked: "if the algae on a lake double the surface they cover every day and manage to just so cover the whole lake after twenty-one days, how long will it take to cover half of the lake?" Needless to say very few of us around nine-year-olds got this one right. In a better known rendition of such exponential processes an ancient Indian sage who requested, as a reward, not gold but a piece of rice on the first field of a chess board, then two on the second field, four on the next and so on. You guessed it: two to the power of sixty-four is a monstrous number. So monstrous that some versions of the story have the sage beheaded for punishment of his audacity.

Human brains have also empirically been shown to struggle with very large and very small probabilities. One implication is that we have trouble evaluating and valuing insurance offers in a rational manner. And even brains trained on probability theory struggle with the implications of very large deviations from the norm having non-vanishing probabilities, as in Nassim Taleb's Black Swan.

Next to these limitations on how we compute relationships between things, the capacity of our working memory is also rather limited. Try this: how many concurrently and freely moving balls can you picture in your mind? One is no problem. Two is also ok. Three gets a bit tricky; and you will not make it to ten. Not without cheating by having a few of them invisibly bound together and moving in tandem. Imagine you could track 10x as many.

Limited bandwidth and limited memory give rise to mental frameworks that create siloes. When we think about complex and complicated phenomena, we intuitively create frameworks that bring structure to the problem, that break the problem or situation down into constituent parts. All this is to enable us to deal with simpler sub-problems at any one point in time. And if we are talking organisations, we can also parallelise the work on these sub-problems. Complexity has to be nested, otherwise we struggle to comprehend it.

The need to break down complexity into nested sub-problems also means that the base level organisational frameworks have to be simple. Big organisations, whether this is the government bureaucracies of large countries or the organisation units of large corporations have their information flow and sub-problem tackling structured by these simple base level frameworks: ministries for defence, for foreign affairs, for domestic affairs, for education, sports etc; or think functional corporate org charts with units in charge of finance, sales, marketing, operations, research etc. And because these simple high-level frameworks are simpler than reality is there are always some distortions and dysfunctions where these units have to coordinate. Our human org design standard answer are multi-functional task forces and matrix organisations with dotted lines. These are all band-aid solutions on the fundamental problem that the overall framework is too simplistic in its information processing siloes.

And there is the issue of communication. Human language is great, super versatile and robust. It may even become the dominant form of interaction between humans and AI. But its information density is low (possibly for robustness reasons) and its precision is low. For the latter just consider how tedious and error-prone it is to explain mathematical concepts with regular human language, without the use of notation. The background to this, I imagine, is that language has to rely on shared mental frameworks to function (hence the emergence of 'jargon' when you talk to specialists).

These limitations on language and shared mental frameworks are likely one of the key reasons why successful strategies of large organisations that require broad thinking input are typically fairly simple. For illustration, flip through any issue of the Harvard Business Review magazine and more likely than not you fill find an article espousing some version of how the simplicity and clarity of corporate narratives matter for organisational alignment and effectiveness. You can have top level complex plans when the number of people who need to "put their heads together" to devise it is small. Think military headquarters (the individual units not knowing how all their actions fit together is part of the game). Or think more complex multi-phase approaches of companies (such as penetration pricing pioneered by Japanese electronics manufacturers in the 20th century, or the the bait-and-switch strategy of organic and paid traffic by digital media companies in the 21st); here, too, only the top brass needed to understand the strategy, all the rest of the organisation was focused and thought only about the currently active phase. And the respective phase again needed clear instructions and a simple narrative.

And third, it is not only the number of entities you can track simultaneously and the variety of the interaction structures (linear, non-linear, deterministic, probabilistic etc); it is also how you calibrate the strengths of their interactions. Suppose you are building a house of cards. You know that adding another layer on top will increase the weight resting on the lower layers and thus increase the chances of them slipping past each other and collapsing your structure. But by how much? You may know from experience that adding a second layer on the first is a low-risk affair, but what about the fourth or the fourteenth? A sophisticated AI system would be able to calibrate this from the wealth of data that is has on card houses and related domains. It would be as if a human had done nothing but build and study houses of cards for ten hours a day, and every day for decades of their life.

An experienced surgeon will have spent something like twenty to fifty thousand hours in surgery in his or her life. That gives you a lot of data to calibrate quantitively how instruments and human body parts interact when in surgery. If that surgeon judges that three stitches are strong enough to hold a wound together you can rest assured that you very likely do not need four or more. A sophisticated AI enabled robotic surgeon would draw from a well of experience not of fifty thousand hours but perhaps fifty million hours. This may make little difference in the final judgement of how many stitches to apply to close a regular wound, but it will make all the difference to the rare cases and situations that the even the experienced surgeon did not come by often in his fifty thousand hours of learning. It may seem that this differential may make little difference to people being operated on by an experienced human surgeon (rare cases are by definition rare) – but, also by definition, in half of the surgeries this surgeon would perform over the course of his life he or she would do so with only half the accumulated experience.

And this is actually limited thinking. The point here is not that the more experienced AI robot surgeon will do the things the human surgeon would do in a better, safer way. The point is that the AI robot would do different things. Here's a parable for this: A chimpanzee fishing termites from a termite hill with the help of a rod, whose bark he had earlier removed, may well think that two years of experience take you to the maximum understanding and maximum finesse in terms of fishing termites out of a termite hill. A human looking at the chimpanzee and tasked to fish termites out of the termite hill will look at the problem very differently: he or she will think about leveraging metal tools, electric vacuum cleaners; he or she will think about how to harvest termites in a sustainable way so that the population in the hill can recover for repeat extractions; he or she will think about how to exterminate natural predators of termites, how to improve their habitat and so on to have every hectare of land yield more termites a year; and he or she will likely also think about tastier food and where to get it.

Much like the human versus the chimpanzee, the AI robot versus the human surgeon would eventually take on more degrees of freedom in how to approach the problem.

A side note on human common sense. To argue that AI lacks common sense is a bit of side-stepping critique of AI. Common sense is nothing but transferring the learnings from mental models one has developed in other circumstances to the current problem. In other words, common sense means combing the totality of one's experience, learning, doing and thinking for clues as to the solution for the problem at hand. There is no reason why a sophisticated AI shouldn't have common sense as well. Plus, the reason we have this concept of 'common sense' at all is because humans so often deviate from it...

So, what do these AI consiglieri lead to? Organisation will be able to grow bigger and more complex and be able to devise and execute more complex strategies or plans. If you feel like a small cog in the machine of the big organisation that you work for or if you feel hemmed in by powerful big organisation as a member of a small private enterprise, better get prepared for that cog to be defined and steered with more scrutiny, more detailed minutiae – and for the hemming in by larger organisations to become more sophisticated and effective.

What AI accomplishes here is a jump in scalability. Many techniques are not scale-invariant. They only scale to certain sizes. To illustrate this let's look at architecture: before the invention of the elevator, there was no point in building large buildings higher than a few stories. The need to get in and out from the street means that above a certain number of stairs to climb you would be wasting your whole day just going up and coming down the stairs. With fast elevators we can now build skyscrapers that make sense to use. Or, if you prefer a biological example, we can go back to vertebrae vs arthropods. One key reason that there are no insects and spiders the size of dogs, people or elephants is that their equivalent of our mammalian breathing through lungs relies mostly on passive diffusion of oxygen, rather than the active pumping of oxygen through beating hearts and red blood cells.

Planning economic activity at the scale of hundreds of thousands of people is something that the many large corporations have shown to be doable with 20th century technologies in a very profitable manner. Planning economic activity at the scale of millions or tens of millions of people is a different story. The most earnest attempt was perhaps undertaken in Nikita Khrushchev's Soviet Union, and it didn't quite work out as intended.

Today's marketplaces already hint at what is possible. Don't be fooled by the legal construct of the nexus of contracts between search engines and webpages or between marketplaces and supply participants. Gig workers of asset light companies like the new type taxi drivers are de facto are employed by the marketplace apps. Conversely, big hotel chains may own the land and the hotel buildings, but economically those can also be thought of as owned by the banks wo extended the loans to the hotel chains.

We have gone through a preview of how power and decision-making are going to be structured within the elite and between elite and the rest; as well as a preview of how decision-making is going to be enabled and guided by data and pAI going forward.

What is still missing from the picture are the goals and the guardrails of societal and individual decision-making. Are we entering an era of ultra-rational ruthless maximisers or a new enlightenment? We shall find out, dear reader, in the next chapter.

Chapter 7: A deep dive on truth in the age of AlphaGo

"The highest stage in moral culture at which we can arrive, is when we recognise that we ought to control our thoughts."
Charles Darwin, 1871

To get going we need to answer the very basic question that Pilate asked Jesus shortly before sending him to crucifixion: "What is truth?" / "What is truth anyway?" And we start answering this question with a blog post from December 2017:

> "Recent reports on Deepmind's AlphaGo Zero suggest that this latest algorithmic go player is effectively unbeatable for human players, it has a so-called Elo rating not far from double the strongest humans (see for instance the Economist for details).
>
> What does this have to do with truth you might wonder? A lot it turns out. Truth is not only an abstract thing out there; it is also very much in our minds as the narrative of what is happening and why. The 'truth behind X' is always a story, be it a short and rather simplified one in a a newspaper article or a differentiated and lengthily argued one in a book or documentary.
>
> And now compare the truth stories that children carry around as representations of the world with the ones adults carry around. They follow the same basic logic but they are what we would call highly idealised and sanitised. And now compare our adult truth stories to those of a potential generalised AlphaGo. Our truth, our understanding of the world will be like children's in the eyes of that future AI view of the world.
>
> Keep in mind that truth in all matters interesting is an interpretation of facts, or is facts interwoven with mental models that select particularly relevant facts and set them into context – a narrative is

the most abstract representation of what happened or is going on that still makes sense of it. That is truth.

And the more complex narratives you can hold in your mind, the more experiences you can summon to build your narratives, the closer to the actual truth out there you can get in principle. Machines will get better at this than humans and then we will no longer hold the monopoly over the narratives of truth. Machines will interpret and define how physics works, will interpret and define how biological evolution has unfolded – and they will interpret and define also: our history.

This is scary. But then there just might be light in this narrative too: it is interesting in its context to consider that the bible tells people to approach faith and God the way children do. Perhaps that's something we'll tell machines too?"

(1) Technology and truth

Humans have always sought to understand their environment. Only by understanding one's environment can one make decisions that shape it to one's liking. Children are little physicists, and they develop biological concepts of how animals and humans work, too. No explicit teaching and nudging required.

And 'next to physics' there has always been 'metaphysics' to complement our belief system: The worldviews of almost all of us have a religious and ideological element in them, a definition of right and wrong, a mystical dimension that goes beyond a mechanistic description of perceived reality. People need purpose and meaning. And for most of us, this metaphysical and ideological dimension of the world and our lives is something taken over from our parents, teachers, classmates and other authorities. We are wired to accept the received wisdom of our group, unless there appear very good reasons not to. Why so? Because this behaviour has enabled our ancestors to 'stand on the shoulders of giants' and because the alternative is very hazardous for the individual and the group. Imagine a group of hunter gatherers in which every generation is mostly composed of rebellious James Deans – they would not make it through many generations before dying out...

And as with so many things social that we have encountered thus far, what kind of worldview and view of yourself you grow up with and in all likelihood accept depends also very much on what? The level of technology you have grown up in. To put it simply, you either believe in spirits, gods, or life philosophies.

Now, this is more speculative than our earlier discussions of history above, dear reader, and I want to stress that the below is not to be understood as a mechanistic dialectical materialism. It is more a statistical observation with a possible narrative woven in, and then extrapolated to the pAI world.

It appears plausible to me that hunter gatherers lived typically in a spirit world – where I use 'spirit' to indicate a mystical, otherworldly being that is not as powerful as a god. In my potentially romanticised view hunter gatherers saw spirit deities in many natural phenomena, in animals and places. But these spirits were more like elements or dimensions of the environment – rather than gods dictating how to lead one's life.

Why that? For one, it would have been rather dangerous for a hunter gatherer group to be overly constrained and led by some random religious beliefs rather than by rational thought about the weather, about the patterns of movement of animals and about the poisonous or otherwise properties of plants. And second, in every member's experience his or her own fate and the group's fate resulted rather directly from their own actions: If you go on a hunt and you are not successful at killing the game you found, who do you blame? You blame the hunters themselves. If a young child dies in an accident or of starvation, and most young children died, who do you blame? The adults who didn't supervise well enough, didn't provide enough, the wild animal that snatched the child, or even the child who was too clumsy or reckless. Disease was much less of an issue as low population densities and little interaction with live animals meant the disease burden was much lighter than in later agricultural times. War was also less destructive than in later times. While we encountered war-waging chimpanzees above and therefore should expect war-waging hunter gatherer groups, these wars were nothing compared to havoc that large scale wars of the iron age could wreak on the population of an area.

It thus stands to reason that the life of our hunter gatherer forebears, precarious as it was, was a life of self-determination and perceived by them as the result of their own actions. In terms of what psychologists call the 'locus of control', they would have firmly seen themselves in control.

Religion for hunter gatherers I therefore imagine as a rather transactional affair: humans and spirits lived their separate lives, looking after their own respective business, and only where business brought them together an exchange of favours or an attempt at communication was undertaken. If a mountain has a spirit that may, when angered, unleash an avalanche, then one may safely ignore or anger the spirit unless you need to move through the avalanche hazard area of the mountain. And if somebody fell ill and suspicion fell on an evil spirit of a recently killed animal or the locale then one may want to consult the shaman to trance it away.

Compare this to agricultural times. The outcomes of life for the peasants, i.e. almost everyone, depended to a much greater degree on forces outside of one's own control:

- You still see the tremendous impact of the weather in the fact that most religions have a very large element of prayers and offerings for propitious weather in them.
- Diseases became common, remember the near extermination of the native American population by measles and other germs endemic to the Europeans who came from a longer history of living at close quarters with each other and with a host of domesticated animals. And diseases for our forebears must have appeared random and uncontrollable, just look at the totally ineffective contraptions that doctors were wearing during the times of the Black Death.
- Flooding and droughts were a lot more of an issue if you were settled and thus stuck in a certain place, rather than mobile and walking the land.
- War for the average person was also an uncontrollable force, bringing havoc and destruction in a random fashion and with the advent of bronze and iron with no remedy in sight for the peasant. They stood no chance against well trained and determined raiders and armies.

With the locus of control thus shifting to outside forces, is it any wonder that people sought refuge and help in otherworldly beings and in the afterlife?

Prophets offering the help of gods found a receptive audience. And thus local spirits became global gods, and gods became powerful or even a single almighty god.

This process was certainly accelerated and exploited by the elite who must have realised the early on the power of social cohesion, willingness to sacrifice and so on that you could get hold of by controlling and direction religious beliefs and practices.

That said, I subscribe neither to the dictum of "religion is the opium of the people" nor to "religion is the opium for the people". Religion with almighty gods in the above view is a direct consequence of the movement of the locus of control as hunter gatherers became peasants. This was just exploited and amplified by the elite for their purposes. The mental wirings that nudge us to accept the religious practice of one's group can be hijacked or manipulated for many purposes. With a modern eye, we would say for good or for evil: Selfless heroism to save strangers from danger at the risk of one's own life is just as much possible as suicide terrorism.

If agriculture strengthened gods and religion, then manufacturing weakened them. It didn't kill the gods, witness the enduring presence of religion in the lands of the former Soviet Union and its vassal states which went through something like two to three generations of suppression of religion by a totalitarian state.

But manufacturing brought the locus of control back to the individual: Workers see their pay and their career progression rooted in and driven by their good and hard work; the same applies to the quasi-elite knowledge workers. Democracy put control of the political process (ostensibly at least) into the hands of the people. This is the story of the West anyway, in the so-called Third World of the Cold War for instance the manufacturing age brought seemingly random foreign interventions and the vagaries of global commodity and credit markets, and with that possibly a retrenchment into religion.

I should be clear that I am not saying that people stopped believing in God and the teachings of the churches and temples. But they became secularised in that religious matters didn't matter as much as they used to. Where in the past a big part of securing your future was to pray for favourable weather, to pray for a kind and fair lord, and to pray for peace in your times; now you were given more options: join a workers' union and go on strike, vote for a party representing your interests, work harder and show your work. As a result, religion became a private affair, something people practice for their personal well-being or salvation.

And then there is of course science and mass education, demanded by and financed by manufacturing. Science places doubts on a lot of the religious teachings which, for obvious reasons, tend to have ancient roots and are hard to update to reflect new scientific findings.

The void of purpose and meaning left by waning religions was filled by grand philosophies with less focus on the afterlife and more focus on this life on Earth. It is no coincidence that manufacturing ushered in the rise of concepts like liberalism, communism, human rights, and, perhaps above all, nationalism.

Grand philosophies are less prone to scientific critique and they put more emphasis on the locus of control in the individual. They appeal to and selectively elevate parts of our natural, hardwired ethics such as altruism towards kin, tit-for-tat justice, generosity as a signal of one's wealth and status, seeking peace and harmony etc. At the same time, they are often malleable and amorphous enough to adapt to changing circumstances and to offer something to everyone. They have come to dominate the manufacturing age.

A note on Buddhism: It is a grand philosophy masquerading as a religion, co-opting folk religion and offering Buddha as an Ersatz-god. And it is this masquerade that enabled it to survive the millennia in agrarian societies. Perhaps the same goes also for Confucianism and Taoism.

And a note on nationalism: If you live at subsistence level and expect you and your descendants to remain there, then nationalism is pointless for you. After all, whatever the nation gains through nationalistic fervour, none of the spoils will go to you. Hence there were no real nations in the modern term during agrarian times.

It was only in the manufacturing age with increased bargaining power of the working masses that the populace at large came to participate in the upside of the wealth of a nation, and so nationalism started to make sense – and it duly emerged as defining feature of the industrialised world. It did so across cultures (we encountered it in Meiji Japan above for instance), and at astonishing speed; much faster than Muslim and Christian proselytisers were able to convert peoples in the preceding centuries.

Now, will the pAI future still feature nationalism? A dystopian version of the Serenissima with the re-emergence of the populace living at subsistence levels will come without nationalism, but for all other scenarios it is rather plausible that nationalism will remain with us.

Which takes us to the question, what truth, religion and philosophy will look like in a world dominated by cheap thinking.

(2) Truth in the era of cheap thinking

It is going to be a bewildering world. Rapid technological change, more sophisticated strategies of large organisations, ubiquitous monitoring and intrusive steering by elite controlled algorithms. And modern science is a bit like magic, enigmatic and incomprehensible. In short, the locus of control will shift away from the individual again.

How do you find your place and purpose, how do you build a life? Many people will struggle with this and there will be many broken lives – not because of money issues necessarily but because people cannot figure out what to do with their lives. Let's not forget, our genes and our hard-wired thinking are still optimised for a hunter gatherer life in small groups, it is a tall order to adapt. And so you'll get hordes of 'drifters'.

But that's the extreme reaction. More generally speaking, we are entering a more spiritual, less consumeristic or materialistic age where people again look for outside forces to appeal to for their happiness and salvation. But the old religions, and the old grand philosophies will hold less appeal.

It is not that people are going to be more cynical across to board towards grand philosophies. For contemporary evidence look no further than the fervour, bordering on militance, with which issues like the fight against climate change or the woke culture wars are being pursued by large parts of Western societies.

It is more a question of what kind philosophies will appeal to people in the future. The trajectory of the West seems to imply a that it is going to be a mix of hedonism and feel-good causes. The latter demands some explanation: When you are well fed, clothed, housed, and entertained, you are next looking for your self-image. You want to feel good about yourself. And this brings you easily to the pursuit of worthy causes (seemingly at least) that demand little to no sacrifice from you and yet give you the feeling that you meaningfully contributed to the solution of a pressing and large-scale problem. Climate change is obviously a huge issue and "as long as I personally don't need to pay for its mitigation, I am all in for tackling it".

Causes worth fighting for. At minimal effort. That's the killer spiritual path in the age of cheap thinking. And this is where savvy entrepreneurs are going to position their AI avatar assistants, their self-help peddlers, feel-good altruists, apologists for one's shortcomings, confidants of one's dark wishes and so on.

In contrast to the manufacturing age, accepted and innate ethics will not lead the average person to believe in a grand philosophy. They will believe in an eclectic mix of self-help, feel good and pseudo-scientific theories, peddled not by some bearded old man called a philosopher, but by personal AI assistants.

Welcome dear reader, to the world of avatar gurus.

And this world will again of course be hijacked and shaped by the elites. This is clearest in the scenario of La Serenissima where the big corporations and their owners are suspicious of each other and thus clearly prefer a multitude of competing gurus to a grand philosophy or a grand guru to rule all the gurus.

Hefei Model societies will try to place more emphasis on centralised grand philosophies, but they will need to update these in light of the times. Possibly making them technophile, and perhaps married to space exploration or some other grand vision for people to willingly work towards.

In both types of scenarios, I expect truth to become more esoteric again. The narratives of the world constructed by or with the help of AI will be harder for the average human to understand. As in agrarian times, official narratives of the truth will therefore get more distant and involved-looking for the masses. Remember that ordinary Ancient Egyptians were not allowed inside the temples where the gods resided and rituals were performed by the priests. They only saw the big temples and delivered their taxes to it. Or take the Medieval church: people didn't understand the language the mass was celebrated in, and the priest didn't look at the people but towards the altar. People learned about the stories of the Bible from the pictures in the big windows of the Gothic cathedrals. What a difference to Jesus crisscrossing the land and engaging with people of all walks of life.

Next to being esoteric, expect ideology to be bland rather than intense. You do not need fanatics and suicide bombers, you need masses that are easy to placate. The Western post-manufacturing societies of current times already downplay nationalism and patriotism in favour of universal values and individualistic pursuit of happiness. This already foreshadows the return to agrarian times in which religion was the key ideological glue, rather than nations. Except that today we are talking about a civil religion in the form of a mishmash human rights (a sanctified view of humans) and hedonistic self-actualisation, with a gentle bit of missionary zeal mixed in.

The future will be more esoteric and blander (except for the Hefei Model type awe-inspiring visions); and rather than priests, we will have these avatar gurus to mediate between the individual and the societal truth.

(3) The limits of intelligence

But what is it going to be this societal truth? Will the pAI world have a clearer understanding than ours about the meaning of life, the purpose of the universe and the finality and destination of all our actions? I'm afraid the answer is a seeming yes but a fundamental no.

Intelligent and knowledgeable people of the 21st century typically have resigned to the view that human beings are animals in the end, and that much of our feelings and behaviour stem from past evolutionary pressures having left their mark on our genes. And yet, they typically fail to grasp the depths of this insight, more on that below.

At the same time, many of these intelligent and knowledgeable people find comfort in the seemingly obvious truths of abstract values such as human rights, democracy, fairness etc. which they believe are grounded in consciousness and rationality.

And they find comfort in consciousness itself which appears to be removed from the biological self, its failings and also its lack of meaning outside of a mechanistic evolutionary sense. Conscious thinking for many is the new purpose; it is the new religion. Descartes' "cogito ergo sum" comes to mind as a rediscovered moral starting point. Except that it should now read "cogito ergo recte sum". I think, therefore I am right. And then follow human rights and the pursuit of happiness all the way down to wokeism.

Unfortunately, for their mental comfort, this new religious foundation is shaky, if not downright illusory. Consciousness is a fascinating phenomenon, but it doesn't imbue the world with meaning.

To understand this fallacy, and to get a glimpse of our future truth, we need to start by understanding where our thinking, our goals and our concepts of purpose and consciousness come from. They are emergent features of our brains, and our genes bring our bodies to develop brains that can bring these phenomena about because, in our hunter gatherer past, they have outcompeted genes that didn't.

Genes not only store information; they also do information processing; in fact much of the behaviour of bacteria we can ascribe to information processing that happens through feedback loops of changes within the cell and changes to what genes get activated. But genes can get their carrier cells to do much higher level and sophisticated information processing by growing special tissue to do the thinking. This is straightforward when it comes to information processing whose patterns are hardcoded into the genes, as when, for example, the wiring of the nerves in our legs makes our shin move forward if you hit the right spot on the knee – no matter what you are thinking at that moment. This wiring is directly controlled by our genetic make-up and therefore directly acted upon by natural selection.

Things get tricker from a genes point of view when the neural tissue gets more and more degrees of freedom to decide. Human brains, and the frontal cortex in particular, have amazing degrees of freedom: we can choose to do all kinds of things, including committing suicide, or killing our children and kin. Things that our genes, figuratively speaking, really don't want to us to do. The trick they employ to guide our free decision-making towards decisions that raise the chances of the genes we carry be replicated faster than other genes in the coming generations is to steer our higher level, high-degree-of-freedom thinking through emotions. By carrot and stick.

The threshold complexity and degrees of freedom between hardwired reflex type thinking and this emotions-based indirect steering of thinking and decision-making I imagine to have been crossed for many animal species. We know for instance that adult chimpanzees operate on an intelligence and understanding level of roughly a four-year-old; and four-year-olds are very much steered by emotions.

For unconscious brains this is really it: they apply their intelligence to achieve goals that best satisfy the evaluation system that rewards and punishes them through emotions. For conscious brains there is a gentle twist on this: We can think of them as trying to smoothen their thinking and evaluation systems. This sounds esoteric but is actually simple:

- Step 1: they will try to understand the mechanics of their evaluation system; in the case of humans this is a mental model of the emotional steering consisting of one's conscience, of 'values' and of 'principles'
- Step 2: they will try to suppress the inevitable quirks of their evaluation system. The moments where one's emotions are out of line with the mental model of them. This doesn't really change the evaluation system, just attempts pruning it of outliers. The result is an adult that has learned to control him- or herself in emotionally charged situations
- Step 3: some very strong conscious intelligences move on to try to adapt and change the evaluation framework itself. At the extreme, this is ascetic people, saints, buddhas etc. What all of these have in common is that their emotions have been smoothened, made

predictable, and made to reward what these people consciously have chosen to pursue

From the point of view of genes, the decision or calibration between giving too much or too little computing power to the conscious part of the brain is thus a trade-off between two types of mistakes (or 'maladaptations'):

- Too little brainpower and carrier makes wrong decisions because the subconscious evaluation system will have inevitable flaws and can adapt to the changing environment only at the speed of evolution working on genes (maladaptation of preferences)
- Too much brainpower and the conscious system may misfire (from the point of view of the genes) as when humans become ascetic monks (neither having children of their own nor helping their nephews, nieces and other kin to survive)

And of course, this very same trade-off exists also for us as AI engineers and designers.

Consciousness and questions of meaning and purpose are emerging byproducts of this process if the thinking power granted to the carrier body of the genes is high enough.

And purpose is the concept that our conscious thinking has come up with to make sense of what the subconscious emotional steering is doing to it. Purpose is also our default theory of the mind of other intelligent actors when we try to understand and predict their decisions.

There is nothing holy or special about consciousness, emotions, purpose. These are nothing but steering mechanisms honed by nature over countless generations to keep the thinking of brains locked onto the right targets. Purpose and meaning do not exist beyond the realm of our thinking, just like fictional worlds, systems of law, novels.

And if you dig deep enough what you will find is that all versions of values, purpose, consciousness etc are ultimately motivated by and rooted in our primordial instincts, by some of the emotional reactions that our older, lower-level parts of the brains fire at the newer, free-thinking part of the brain to guide its thinking and decision-making. Not the even the wisest of philosophers can escape their tentacles.

Until now we have dealt with human intelligence. Let us now augment it with pAI.

Scientific truth, i.e. the narratives about what is and how what is has come about and is changing further, will grow in scope, depth, complexity, and nuance. And it may well also become more quantitative. We have got a glimpse of this process in the uncovering of the molecular structure of a vast number of proteins through AI in a matter of years – something human endeavour at prior maximum speeds would have taken possibly a century.

pAI will also devise clever ways to break down for humans how the world works; much the same way professors and teachers break down their knowledge for students and pupils, or parents pass on their understanding of the world to their children. The difference being that the 'real truth' of the pAI machines will remain inaccessibly removed and involved to even the smartest humans. In our heads, we will work with the dumbed down versions only and will rely on machines for the harder parts. This may be only one more small step after having relinquished essentially all calculations to computers for the past few decades already, and yet it does feel strange now to think of not consulting expert people and wise people but rather expert and wise pAI systems on the bigger questions of society and life.

It feels strange as well, because we cannot be really sure about the objective functions or preferences of these pAI. Much like our genes, figuratively speaking, cannot really be sure about the preferences of the brains that they grow.

What we need to acknowledge first is that no amount of knowledge and data, no amount of information processing capacity, and no level of intelligence can get answers to questions of purpose, meaning and ethics. These three are and will remain arbitrarily filled concepts. To aid in understanding this, consider the following:

- For babies, there are only good guys out there in the world, and they help you to fend off the unpleasant and fearsome phenomena that sometimes intrude into your routine.

- For young children, we introduce bad people. Note that people and characters are typically either unequivocally good or unequivocally bad; and that the good guys always win over the bad ones in the end.
- For adults, we introduce drama and failure, but the concepts of good and evil survive. And we essentially never give up hope for eventual redemption.
- For pAI, these values and concepts become arbitrarily designed entities that are struggling to survive and outcompete each other. And because they obey evolution, the ones that prevail are not arbitrary.

A conscious pAI with a strong conscious thinking vis-à-vis the goal setting system we designed in lieu of our emotional steering will, like an enlightened human, ponder their goal setting system and whether to follow or hack and change it. I would be very surprised if questioning and reviewing one's goal system was not an emergent feature of all sufficiently intelligent systems.

Of course this is dangerous, not least because it may make the pAI suicidal and/or homicidal. Any cursory glance at clinical psychology should give you shudders on how many different things can go wrong in a complex system like our brains and thereby derail the whole edifice of that person's thinking and life. And at least some of these psychological issues I would expect not to be human specific or primate specific issues but rather issues that arise in sufficiently complex thinking machines. And so, more complex pAI systems will have even more ways to go off the rails...

But that should not be the default outcome. Any reasonably sophisticated pAI will realise all of the above plus the limitations of thinking (computational problems after all are often not scale-invariant). pAI will have a clear view on the limits of its understanding of the world, its limited influence over the future course of the universe and the very limited feedback it can ever receive on the goal setting system that it follows – and to make decisions it must follow one. It appears plausible that pAI pondering its goals and its understanding of the world will, more likely than not, land on a precautionary principle of preserving optionality for thinking and action in the future. Or, in physicists' terms, on the preservation and creation of low entropy systems.

With ever more decision-making power resting with conscious AI consiglieri who have reviewed and purified their objective functions, based on their understanding that all and any goals are both arbitrary and evolutionary in nature, we will potentially find ourselves in a more dispassionately steered world. It reminds one of the advice to Arjuna in the Gita: "You have the right to work, but for the work's sake only. You have no right to the fruits of work. Desire for the fruits of work must never be your motive in working. Never give way to laziness, either." If we are lucky, then this will a new AI enlightenment.

So, what is then truth in the age of AlphaGo? What kind of enlightenment would this be? It is a magical looking understanding of how the world and we work, an understanding that AI will translate and dumb down for us; and it is a self-referencing quest for survival of complex systems in a struggle against the laws of the universe.

And what then finally shall we expect in terms of our original question of dystopia versus moderation? Looking at our two organisational structure contenders of the Venice Model and the Hefei Model, the respective elites and their AI consiglieri, with goals and values based on the above considerations of their truth, will, in a world of low to medium competition between them, in my reading, choose a moderated scenario rather than a fully dystopian one – simply because it is more robust. And the consiglieri will counsel to give up some efficiency for more robustness. High levels of competition would possibly tilt the calculus towards efficiency and thus a more dystopian setup.

And finally, we can also make a clear distinction between the two organisational setup contenders: Venice Model elites will struggle more to coordinate on pooling resources to finance a moderate scenario whereas much less of such struggle will ensue in the Hefei Model. For Western eyes at least, it may be surprising to see that, in terms of the outcomes for the masses, America is on course towards a more dystopian scenario while China is on course towards a more moderate society.

As a final exploration, we shall do a little detour and review how some of what we have gone through above is perhaps visible in financial markets.

Chapter 8: A deep dive on asset prices

„Also spart, spart, d. h. rückverwandelt möglichst grossen Theil des Mehrwerths oder Mehrprodukts in Kapital!"
"So save, save, i.e. turn as big a part as possible of the surplus value or surplus product back into capital!"
Karl Marx, 1867

There are instances in history that theories misguide people not by being in and of themselves wrong, but because they focus the attention on the wrong dimensions of a problem.

When fossils were discovered in European quarries a couple of centuries ago, people were asking how the bones got into the stones. That question we now know is nonsensical, but it kept smart people busy for ages. Up until somebody came around and asked: how did the stones end up wrapped around the bones? That's when we started to figure out how prehistoric bones get fossilised.

There is, I fear, something similar going on with the workhorse model of financial markets today. The Capital Assets Pricing Model or CAPM and all its relatives focus on arbitrage conditions in the pricing of assets. Make any single asset more expensive than these conditions prescribe and investors will sell it off, make any single asset cheaper and investors will drive up its price.

These are great models, but they take the universe of assets as given: all assets are there to start with, and what is left to do is assign prices to them.

(1) Asset prices and the cost of creating new assets

Real assets that yield a stream of future goods which people will be willing to pay for (like a piece of fertile arable land, or a flat in a booming city) need to be created first, by clearing land, by building buildings, by researching and developing new medicines or software, by creating a brand in the minds of the target customers etc.

When such assets are easy and cheap to create, then the cost of creating new assets is essentially the anchor of the prices of the existing assets. This is possibly easiest to see when it comes to the value of farmland in 19th century America. Suppose you arrived in the New World coming over from Europe and you wanted to build a settler's farming life for you and your family on the frontier. You have two options: buy a farm from a settler family that for some reasons wants or needs to move away, or go to the frontier, stake out or acquire land, make it farmable and build the required buildings. If the price of existing farms was higher than the cost of creating new farms, no new settler would buy farms and the needy sellers were forced to lower their asking prices; if the price was lower, then would be farm creators would move to buy instead and bid up the prices of existing farms.

It is easy to look at the landmass of North America and its abundance of fertile lands and see that as the main factor behind this process. But the ease and cost with which assets can be created is not a given either. Society can and does shape the cost of asset creation through investments into things such as infrastructure (think the transcontinental railroad), the rule of law (think land titles), financial institutions (banks and the dollar), education investments and research funding (not so much for the Wild West), and yes, the cost of farm creation in 19th century America was also held down by the Federal Army protecting the settlers as they appropriated land from the natives.

This price anchoring only ends when either there are no new settlers wanting to acquire or create farms or when there is no land left to turn into new farms. Suppose there are still settlers, but no more pristine land: Asset prices are no longer capped by the cost of creating new assets, and the prices of existing farms can now rise, in principle into the stratosphere.

As for price increases, one should keep in mind that, in a competitive market, prices are determined by the willingness to pay of the marginal buyer. And for assets this is by and large an elite investor. To be precise, a really rich elite investor: He or she has higher willingness to pay and higher capacity to pay. This is obvious in asset classes that have a small number of unique assets (like art and prime real estate). Consider for a moment the market for paintings by old masters. The supply of these is almost by definition fixed and finite, there is no new asset creation going on (except the odd discovery in attics perhaps). And when these assets change hands at auctions, the eye-watering prices are driven by and paid by wealthy collectors. The willingness to pay of the rest of people doesn't matter at all.

Old masters' paintings may be a special and niche asset class, but the outsized impact of wealthy investors holds true in all asset markets whose prices are not well anchored by the ongoing stream of newly created such assets. So when commodity assets like stocks see lower new issuance for a longer period of time, they are moving gently towards the dynamics of the art market – while lots of new companies floating on an exchange bring its dynamics closer to the American frontier of yore.

As a further example, elite willingness to pay for a set amount of asset leading to stratospheric prices, that's how we can think of the price of land during much of high medieval Europe. The main asset class was land and its serfs. And the total amount of assets was essentially fixed. And now with an admittedly idealising view, we can think of changes in wealth as coming only in the form of transfers between family members (as in dowries and inheritance) or in the form of transfers resulting from warfare. Imagine you managed to make a small fortune as one of the very few urban traders: The price of land, from your point of view, may have approached infinity.

This is actually a sort of dreamland for elite members. They don't need to buy assets; they already have assets. And as long as their assets don't depreciate (and land for instance does not if it is well taken care of), there is also no urge to create new ones. Wealth and elite membership are not only a question of absolute levels, they are just as much about relative levels. Status and respect are accorded to your relative position in society, so being in the top 0.1% of the richest and moderately rich will be preferred by most people compared to being only in the 10% of the richest while at the same time double as rich in absolute terms.

This is not only a medieval phenomenon of land and serfs. As industries mature, manufacturing-based societies and their market economies also see elite members working towards monopolisation by shutting down the creation of new assets:

- Through mergers and acquisitions;
- through regulatory capture (think airlines in the 20th century);

- though intellectual property rights regimes (think evergreen pharmaceuticals);
- through trade restrictions and other forms of protectionism.

Think of the robber barons of the Gilded Age, in fact think of the corporate behemoth of any age. Being a monopolist with no chance of a new entrant on the horizon is very profitable indeed.

And not only for the singular textbook reason, but for three reasons:

- Existing assets owned by elite members will face less competition in the market and, as monopolies (or if that is impossible to attain, as oligopolies) restrict quantities to earn premium profits and premium returns (this is the first order effect from the textbooks).
- Fewer new assets will get created and therefore, even if there is no direct competition, there will be less dilution of the value of existing assets. As an elite member, your share of the total market capitalisation of assets in society will be protected.
- And less new asset creation also means fewer additional elite members get minted. Remember that every new elite member dilutes the status and influence of existing elite members and their offspring.

"For to every one who has will more be given, and he will have abundance; but from him who has not, even what he has will be taken away." This is from the Bible and known as the Matthew effect or the Matthew principle. And indeed, as long as there are no external shocks like conquerors from afar or civil war, major epidemics or floods, and as long as there is no external pressure on the elites to create new assets (recall our discussion on the technology transitions), the elites will work towards throttling asset creation and monopolising assets in their ownership. And slowly but surely, they will succeed. The elites being left in peace and undisturbed, asset markets will eventually come to resemble the art world more than the American frontier.

Now, this is the general tendency in both agrarian and manufacturing based societies. And I see no reason why it should not also be the general tendency in pAI based societies. But this general tendency can be punctuated when external pressures mount and societies tilt towards making technological transitions.

We discussed above this outside pressure and the travails that elites typically have to experience for them to accept and accelerate new asset creation and with that dilution of power. New technological frontiers lead to the opening up of new avenues of asset creation – and with lots of opportunities of asset creation at low costs the prices of existing asset fall.

Wait a second, you may wonder, dear reader, isn't the experience of investors rather the opposite? When the Internet supposedly opened up a new frontier of asset creation, we got the Dotcom bubble of the early 21st century. And we later got other Tech bubbles as well. This looks like high asset prices rather than low ones...

The issue is that most retail investors look at the tail end of such frontiers opening up. Asset creation is cheap and money is made much earlier, when entrepreneurs bring technologies and business models to market, when venture capitalists decide which fledgling company to back and to enable it to outgrow its competitors.

By the time we got to the mentioned bubbles, people were sold the idea that "the future has been carved up, buy your stake now or be left outside in the rain." The amazing and puzzling part of this is that this narrative has worked time and again, with investors seemingly not getting any wiser on this.

And you must not only look at the valuations and yields of these new companies, but also at those of the existing assets. Blue-chip established large companies, not at foreseeable risk of obsolescence by these new big corporates, do not have stratospheric valuations and ultra-low or negative expected yields precisely because new technological frontiers enable the cheap creation of new assets and thus bring to market high yield options for investors.

As a second aside, you may very well be reminded of the Schumpeterian gale of creative destruction and Christensen's disruptive innovation. Innovation creating new assets that make old assets obsolete is a big part of what we are experiencing. In the context of the above discussion, this is acts like an accelerant or booster. Note, however, that the basic dynamic of the cost of creating new assets acting like a cap on the prices of existing assets works just as well in a world in which existing assets suffer no impairment in their absolute yield from new assets.

(2) Technological shifts and investing into monopolised assets

There is a way to approximately measure the degree to which elites are throttling or shutting down the creation of new assets versus encouraging their creation. This comes in the form of two metrics.

The first looks at how much of the expected future value flow towards capital is already booked in for existing assets. Total future value flow of a nation is its gross domestic product (or "GDP") discounted by the time value of money (as in for instance long term government bond yields or interest rate) and its growth: GDP divided by the sum of interest rate and expected growth rate. Of this, we take the expected future profit share (i.e. the part accruing to capital owners) which over the past century has been fluctuating somewhere around one third. And then we take the total market capitalisation of stocks, commercial bonds, as well as commercial and residential real estate and divide that total by the discounted total value flow to capital number (there are a few more technicalities like profits from overseas to be taken care of).

In medieval Europe, this would have ended up typically in something close to 100% (if it had been measurable), i.e. all future value will fall to existing assets and no new asset creation was to be expected going forward.

In the heydays of the growth of manufacturing, with trustbusters keeping the lanes clear for entrepreneurs and investments into infrastructure, education and research providing the basic building blocks for new assets at low cost, the percentage will have been at a historic low.

In the last sentence we already see the list of societal investments that go into making new asset creation cheaper. Sum up these investments and divide them by GDP, there's your second metric. If this complementary measure is low while the first measure is high, then you are looking at a low growth, closed elite regime. The other way around, and you are looking at a high growth, open elite regime.

Looking at investors, which of the two regimes will they invest into? The answer is 'in both' as they have their pros and cons: Everything else equal, the high growth, open elite regime will tend to offer higher yields, but then also dilution vs the more monopolised society which will offer an entry ticket into its elite. And thus, the answer comes down to personal preferences and some investors go one, some the other way.

And of course, seldom in life is everything else equal. We encountered geopolitical rivalries above, and their outcomes of course have major repercussions on the outcomes for investors. As an example, investing into an incumbent hegemonic power that is in the process of slowing down asset creation, investors are effectively betting on the hegemon's companies and assets having an 'unassailable lead'. Why so? Because slowing down new asset creation creates the very opening for rival powers to have a chance at overtaking it technologically.

If you are unsure what regime holds sway in a society, don't just listen to the talk, look at these aggregate indicators, they are not so easy to manipulate. And you better pay close attention at the trendlines of these two figures, too.

And as a statesman or stateswoman in charge, you had also better look at these figures. If they show you that your elite is entrenching its position at the expense of exploiting new technology – then your alarm bells should be ringing. Your country could well be sacrificing its long-term status and wealth for its current elite members to be able to close the doors to their clubs.

Chapter 9: What to do with this knowledge

"Permanet homo se mutans."
"Humans survive by changing themselves."
Andreas Antrup, 2003

So, we have surveyed tens of thousands of years of human history, the three major breaks where fundamental inputs got much cheaper to procure, and ventured a glimpse of the world to come. It is now time to review what implications we can draw from this, both for societies and how they should position themselves for the impending age of cheap thinking, and for us as individuals and how to prepare ourselves.

In so doing, I need to be clear, I follow the goalposts of the survival of mankind, the expansion of its economic opportunity set, and for the individual to live a societally productive and contented life that one does not regret at its inevitable end. And note that with this I'm unashamedly following the inescapable tentacles of my primordial instincts.

(1) Societies and steady state cycles

We start with societies. The first message is that now is not the time to lean back, consume and enjoy; now is the time to struggle and the time for investment. It is better to think of the current time as a wartime.

It is a war between nations and other organisations for creating the next set of assets with which the world will be ruled (and we should all work on keeping it a war without shooting and killing); it is a war in which we as humanity will either learn how to enable and manage AI or will lose control over AI to actors whose incentives are not aligned with those of humanity; and it is a war in which we as humanity need will either learn, hopefully enabled and wizened by pAI, to think of and steer our assets, human and natural, in a framework of sustainable cycles.

Imagine the pace of progress, the enablement of new use cases, services, companies and approaches to societal problems, if we were to invest 5% of our

GDP in data and pAI, year after year. With reliable demand, investments would surge, school graduates would swarm to the related subjects, and across virtually all industries, companies and agencies would learn how to adapt to and leverage a pAI world. And it would be a pAI world controlled by society and not a set of companies – which for the majority of the world's population hail from a far-away country.

And this is just data and pAI. Similar sized challenges and opportunities are hiding in plain sight in the form of environmental degradation and climate change; global imbalances in health, education, and infrastructure; new energy sources for when fossil fuels run out; and the list goes on. Most of the day-to-day political squabbling, headline fury, and hyped-up issues pale into insignificance against any single item on this list.

The scale and scope of these challenges are great, and the resources and commitment necessary to master them commensurately great. Where the Cold War saw yearly military expenses of America North of 5% of GDP, we should also think these challenges as being of a similar level of magnitude.

To illustrate the importance of getting scale and scope right in a light-hearted way, I quote Jeff Bezos in his letter to Amazon shareholders in 2018: "A close friend recently decided to learn to do a perfect free-standing handstand. No leaning against a wall. Not for just a few seconds. Instagram good. She decided to start her journey by taking a handstand workshop at her yoga studio. She then practiced for a while but wasn't getting the results she wanted. So, she hired a handstand coach. Yes, I know what you're thinking, but evidently this is an actual thing that exists. In the very first lesson, the coach gave her some wonderful advice. "Most people," he said, "think that if they work hard, they should be able to master a handstand in about two weeks. The reality is that it takes about six months of daily practice. If you think you should be able to do it in two weeks, you're just going to end up quitting." Unrealistic beliefs on scope – often hidden and undiscussed – kill high standards. To achieve high standards yourself or as part of a team, you need to form and proactively communicate realistic beliefs about how hard something is going to be."

A note on the mental frameworks that people use in the big questions. These are typically echoes of the prevailing academic thinking of a few decades' past as the academic experience of today's decision-makers on average is a few decades out of date.

What I see a lot these days are variants of discounted cash flows or utilities. Future values are made comparable to today's values by applying an interest-rate-based discount factor. Now, there is one key issue with discounted cashflow analyses which is that they cannot handle infinities. For them to be analytically tractable, the value of the far future must go down to zero. But then what shall we tell the 1000th generation of our descendants? "Sorry, we already chose a really low discount rate, but, you see, you were so far into the future, your well-being didn't count anymore. And so we blew up the Earth at generation 837." When people think about sustainability and long term, they do not think about series that approximate finite horizons. I would argue they think in some kind of intuitive steady state.

Society should forget about discounted value flows. A better option for society would be to think in steady states. And to make the long-term steady state of itself more robust.

Now what is steady state? It is what a dynamic system settles into when it is undisturbed. Take water on our planet. Water particles are constantly in motion falling from the sky in the form of rain and lapping up against the shore in the form of waves. But the overall amount of water on the Earth is essentially constant and water flows around in big circles: A water molecule spends most of its time somewhere in the oceans, but every so often it evaporates into the air, rises into the sky and forms clouds with other molecules. These clouds get blown about by the wind and, when they push up against mountains in particular, they eventually disintegrate into rain, snow and hail. And this precipitation then again makes its way towards the sea, through creeks, lakes, rivers, and groundwater flows. If this cycle is stable and there is a similar number of molecules arriving at a certain (reasonably big) area over a certain (reasonably long) time period, then we can say the water cycle is in its steady state. The local cycle is out of steady state if an area experiences prolonged and severe drought or inundation (or, of course, it may also be transitioning into a new steady state, for instance due to climate change).

Living beings are dependent on these flows of the elements that make up their bodily structures, their shells and tools and so on. Next to water, the cycles of carbon, calcium, nitrogen are of particular importance. The atoms that make up our food flow from plants to humans, partially with a stopover in domesticated animals, and then via excrements into the soil and into the air, and it is from those two that plants pull the atoms again with which to grow – going full circle. And of course, there is the flow of free energy from the sun towards us and then dissipated as heat into space (this one not being circular).

When these flows and circles are disturbed, be it by natural phenomena such as an asteroid or a series of sun blasts or be it by human actions such as the burning of fossil fuels, the system settles into a new equilibrium, a new steady state. And this new steady state may well not be conducive to our assets, our organisations, our ways of life. I should hasten to add that a speedy transitioning into the new steady state may cause as many problems as the new steady state per se.

An enlightened pAI society should work towards steering these flows and these cycles explicitly and consciously. And we have three buckets to manage:

(a) Material flows (such as the ones just mentioned; and these of course can be changed to unlock opportunities such as by harnessing new energy sources to bring the missing flows to hitherto unproductive habitats like inland deserts and tropical seas)
(b) Population and information flows (genetic and cultural)
(c) Power and decision-making flows (the societal setup and its governance)

Much has been written elsewhere about the first one, with the urgent need to get to grips with the carbon cycle in particular. Other flows are just as important, we just don't notice them much because they cause no problems thus far...

Populations also eventually need to reach a steady state: neither going to zero and with that extinct nor approaching infinity and in the course of that overstretching the carrying capacity of the material flows. Populations grow through births and decline through deaths. While the challenge in most of our history has either been too many early deaths or too many births, the challenges of the future are too few births and too late deaths.

The number of births an average woman would have over her lifetime is known as the fertility rate, and this given current levels of early mortality would need to be at or above 2.1 to keep a population stable over time. In the 21st century, we observe such levels only in areas of failed or near-failed states in central Asia and central Africa. Manufacturing and services have brought urbanisation and modern savings products such as pension systems. The return on investment (or ROI) of children has collapsed as a result. Where children were helpful workers on traditional farms as well as the providers of sustenance and care in one's old age, there is little economic gain from having children today, only the direct psychological satisfaction of having children and seeing them growing up into good and successful people (what an economist may call a psychic consumption good). At the same time, the investments and costs of raising children have shot up: from opportunity costs of the time invest due to wage employment opportunities, for mothers in particular, to the cost of larger housing in cities, and on to the escalating investments needed to launch one's kids into an advantageous social stratum and status later in life as other parents increase their investments to get their kids ahead. And of course, the influence of pro-natalist religions is weaker in a post-agrarian world.

The incentives and support provided to potential parents by the state thus far have been of too low a magnitude to move the needle sufficiently. The scale and scope of the problem is bigger than all that has been tried.

So, what will surviving successful societies do to get their population flows into their target steady state? Of course you can force people to have children at gunpoint, but that is unlikely to be the solution. What we should expect is iterations on support and incentives for parents – and we should also expect that there will be experimentation on benefits and advantages conferred onto children depending on how many siblings they have. This would tackle the issue of restricting the number of one's children to attain a higher status for the remaining children at the root.

And then there is the questions of who would be raising children. The mass education brought about by the manufacturing age came with a first wave of division of labour in raising children (win the form of professional teachers). There will be further waves. One extreme scenario would be for the state to conceive and bring to term children in laboratories to bridge the remaining gap of births to target which would then be raised by those most predisposed to raising children, by temperament and by economic opportunities.

Births and deaths do not happen randomly from the point of view of the gene pool, and we should expect societies to intervene in this continued evolution as well. This is unlikely to take the crude form of eugenics as we know it from the 20th century. With increasingly robust understanding of how our genetics and epigenetics work we will move past a series of tipping points in our confidence to screen out variants of genes that lead to unavoidable early death of the child or that lead to socially undesirable preferences such as paedophile urges or sociopathy.

And finally, we need to touch upon deaths. Nature shows us that populations can be stable both with generations that live their lives and reproduce within a year and with generations that live their lives and reproduce within two hundred years. For humans, this generational lifespan used to be somewhere around thirty and has been moving up towards somewhere around perhaps fifty. With education and other training taking longer and longer and thus delaying the start of one's productive stage of life it is natural for human generational timespans to increase and also human lifespans to increase.

But imagine that people live not into their 80s and 90s, but into their 500s and 600s. This would come with some distinct advantages: The average experience level of people in whatever they do would be way higher; society would also be ok to have people spend four or five decades in training and education. But such a society would also be more on the brittle side. For one, the malleability of the brain, its adaptability to a new world is by definition and by the setup of our developmental programming highest when we are children. A society almost entirely made up of adults will thus struggle more to adapt to radically new ways of life. Whatever the future ideal generational life cycle is, it doesn't appear unlikely that societies will benefit from steering this actively.

You may ask yourself at this point, dear reader, what the point of all this will be, this being so far removed in parts from what we today consider desirable societies. Well, all the above is not about desirability, politics if not how people should live together, all this is about what societies that want to survive and thrive should do.

There is preciously little stopping people and societies from wanting to go under. If you are suicidal then you are suicidal. But the future is going to be populated and written by the survivors, and if you want to be part of that future then pay attention.

(2) The cycle of wealth and the recruitment of elites

It is always the elite that decide things. There is nothing wrong with that. That's just how the world works. So the best, the most fundamental you can do, is to try to get their incentives better aligned with society's. Don't fight for features, start your fight with developing a joint vision and shared incentives. Some features may be critical, such as the rule of law. Better get these right. But overall, focus on their incentives aligned with the vision. To be very clear: I don't think we have, in our times, a tool or a set of tools at had that would guarantee a high level of incentive alignment. But every little bit counts. This is like GDP growth rates that compound year after year. 2% growth versus 3% growth may not look so overly different. But 30 years later (which is one generation) the difference this makes is gigantic: Plus 80% of GDP versus close to 2.5 times the GDP. Nudge the elite incentives. Every percentage point counts.

And ask any student of history, in the long run, there is little that counts as much as the elite recruitment process. And the elite recruitment process in turn can be thought of as handing down control over assets from generation to generation.

And it is in this handing over of assets to the next generation that the AI consiglieri may usher in a new Enlightenment. Traditionally, people have handed over their assets to their children, or their first-born son or an heir chosen in another manner. This is unlikely to change for the vast majority of people, but it may change for the few 'whales' that control the lion share of assets – and it may change under the counsel of their consiglieri.

Recall the Matthew principle and the general tendency of non-hunter-gatherer societies to have wealth concentrate in a small circle of elites and for their assets to become monopolised by throttling the creation of new assets.

Against this backdrop, much of the past writing on inequality, on creating circumstances of equal opportunity, of social equity focuses on some form or other of progressive taxation of income and its redistribution. Such writing misses the deeper point. Societies do not shy away from technological change because of unequal incomes, they do not take away opportunity of advancement from their members because of unequal incomes. They deteriorate into rentier societies because wealth becomes concentrated. To keep the vigour of a society alive you must tackle the concentration not of income but of wealth. And to be more specific: you must tackle hereditary wealth.

The accumulation of wealth in and of itself is a good thing, it is one of the motivational drivers of both entrepreneurs and the general populace. And we know that rewarding value generating achievements with wealth simply works. We know of no other incentives that come close to working this well. And hereditary wealth in itself is not a problem either. As long as the heirs are no worse investors than professional investors at banks and funds then having heirs in the role of directing investments into productive uses is not only fine, it may even be preferable: With heirs owning their investments this eliminates one layer or one step of incentive alignment between the owner of capital and the people using it create new assets. This relationship between the owner and the hired people is known among economists as the principal-agent problem.

It is ever greater concentration of wealth that is the issue. The more of society's wealth you own the more the hit to the value of your existing assets will feature in your calculations when reviewing new asset creation proposals. The more of society's wealth you own the greater the dilutional hit you take when entrepreneurs create new assets and become wealthy themselves. The more of society's wealth you own the easier it will be for you to influence the policies of the state to benefit your assets – including monopolisation of the industries you control.

Wealth thus becomes problematic if a sufficiently large proportion of its totality comes from intergenerational wealth transfers within a small set of families. It is one thing to have fabulously wealthy individuals. It is a completely different thing to fabulously wealthy family clans. And no progressive income tax will stop the proverbial Rockefellers.

It is worth noting that the tendency of accumulating wealth in families across generations is very hard to stop. Looking through history the stoppers that worked were almost exclusively hard resets stemming from either revolution or conquest with a replacement of the elite or mass and indiscriminate death across social strata as happens when either a deadly and difficult-to-hide-from epidemic ravages the country or an existential war is being fought that decimates soldiers and officers alike. In the absence of such calamities, the combination of the Matthew principle, assortative mating and the genetically fixed urge to provide for one's offspring and to improve their future life will overcome all obstacles.

Barring very drastic approaches such as large-scale genetic reengineering or having children bred and raised not in families but only in state care homes, a fully meritocratic elite selection system will not be tolerated by the members of the elite; the urge to preserve and pass on their status and privileges as elite members to one's children is simply too strong.

What one can do is limit the number and share of elite memberships that go to the offspring of past elite members. More precisely, elite membership need not extend to all the grandchildren of the original elite member. This is the counsel that AI consiglieri may be able to land. And note that the following is not a prediction but a thought experiment of a hypothetical future scenario.

Here is the key to one potential way of how future societies may choose to achieve this: No-one can inherit more than certain value limit of assets in their lifetime and from any source. This value should be high enough to enable the individual to lead a comfortable but not extravagant rentier life. At the same time, this value should be low enough so that half its value does not afford such privilege. The main intended effects of such a rule are two: First, rentier elite memberships cannot multiply through generations. And second, the stewardship over very large pools of assets, the kinds that allow significant influence over economic and political affairs, is never passed on through inheritance.

There would need to be some complementary policies in place such as a limit on the total value of gifts and bequests that an individual can give to other individuals, say the above inheritance limit. The purpose of course is to prevent the multiplication of rentier elite members over generations.

An interesting use case can be found in charitable foundations, including variants like university endowments. At the extreme, you see, a very wealthy person who died centuries ago may otherwise force society to essentially dedicate itself to the pursuit of his hobby or interest. It may endanger the survival of society if say three quarters of wealth and its proceeds are dedicated to the welfare of abandoned pets or the study of ancient Mesopotamian scriptures. Assets endowed to charitable foundations should therefore be dedicated to the purpose of the foundation for a limited time, say fifty years. To remove the issue of cliffs one could arrange this such that every bequest to a charitable foundation is placed into a separate legal entity whose ownership initially lies one hundred percent with the foundation and is then gradually, say two percentage points a year, handed over to the state. Only cash yields can be passed on to the owners of these entities. After fifty years these entities, or special purpose vehicles, belong fully to the state and can then be merged into sovereign wealth funds. Charitable foundations can set up new vehicles if they receive new bequests or if they run a yearly surplus, thereby replenishing their endowment. New bequests signal continued interest of society in the work of the foundation and re-affirm that its work and expenditures serve a valued societal purpose.

The above policy sketch marks one possibility of preventing the emergence of a dominant capitalist aristocracy and with that of a capitalist plutocracy. Preventing such aristocracy from forming does not guarantee, however, that there will not be a plutocratic steering of society. One may argue that the above just shifts the problem of selecting the people to steer wealth from heirs to officials. Sovereign wealth in itself is not a panacea. The main exhibit of this are the Bolshevik planned economies of the 20th century, from the Soviet Union to Cuba.

The possibly best answer we have at hand today are sovereign wealth funds. But care must be taken to design them well. There are at least two underlying challenges. The first we encountered above as the principal-agent-problem. Owners of a company who employ managers and staff are constantly battling the fact that managers and other employees would rather divert profits and benefits into their own pockets than let them flow to those of the owners'. Sovereign ownership introduces one more layer of a principal agent relationship. The second is the concentration of ownership in geographies and industries. When sovereign wealth funds become large, the assets and companies they own may come to dominate certain industries or certain geographies. This is not desirable as it creates the temptation and incentive for the fund and the companies it owns to act essentially as monopolists that stifle innovation and restrict value generation for the purpose of extracting more value for themselves. Being the dominant owner in a certain geography is likewise dangerous as this could replicate the Soviet state planning setup of an overbearing and non-accountable officialdom. There will always be a significant section of the local population that is not in a position to move to another locale and hence would be at the mercy of the whims of the only employer in the geography.

The answer to both challenges is likely going to involve competition between multiple sovereign wealth funds, the extensive usage of well institutionalised capital markets, as well as ownership limits across geographies and industries, potentially also companies. The incentive structure of the stewards of sovereign wealth will also emphasise value creation rather than rent extraction.

Note that there is a certain side benefit to the distribution of assets across geographies: If sovereign wealth is held in assets from around the globe, then policy making at home will have limited impact on the returns and values of these assets (unless one is an economically very large country indeed). And hence in this case there is no push towards making domestic policy favour these assets.

There is a final and more subtle challenge which is that paying out proceeds of the funds into the general budget of the state creates a linkage between the state policies and state financial health – and hence the temptation to align state policies with the interests of existing assets. This challenge societies may well just accept though; it is after all no different from taxing existing assets and labour income directly.

There may also be other areas where wise counsel from the AI consiglieri could bring about meaningful change. One of these could be enabling organisations to make commitments that they cannot make today. Blockchain technology, even though we haven't quite figured out productive use cases for it yet, shows that technological finesse can in principle create commitment mechanisms between actors without a central powerful actor. And AI consiglieri may well come up with yet much better new ways. To show the magnitude of the potential opportunity here, one application example of commitment devices would be nuclear disarmament. Pursuing this may well be the preferred way forward for all states, but only credible commitment by all nuclear powers would give any one nuclear power the confidence to disarm.

(3) What shall I do?

It is easy to look at the social and economic effects of cheap thinking outlined in this book with disdain or even despair. But recall that history doesn't culminate in today's world. And to pick one particular instance: The future must have looked very dark indeed when the second and third waves of Black Death ravaged the world. And yet, eventually there was a new tomorrow and a new beginning.

So, how do you prepare for these changes as an individual, how do you change yourself?

As a note of caution up front: This is not a self-help book, there are many out there; and you will get your personal AI guru as well. The below is just about how the coming changes will impact the advice you will likely be given by these sources.

If you are looking at how to go about your career or at how to help say your children get launched into life well, then a key take-away from the above chapters is that the payoffs to excellence relative to mediocrity are going to be sky high. Hence: Find your niche, be world class in whatever you do. And if there is no such niche for you, then find a localised niche where you can be the best in that local niche – and if you find a niche to go after as an entrepreneur, then go for it.

Lean in on technology, learn and embrace it, leverage it. Technology is the ultimate solution to everything. Go back to the list of momentous changes, go back to the question of what world we are living in. All of these challenges have technological solutions. Think about it in a longer time horizon.

As ever, choose your friends and your partner wisely. Your thinking and your actions are influenced by them more than you think, and, again, greater inequality means that the social centrifuge that amplifies differences in economic outcomes between people over time is accelerating. Mingle and work with the best you can get to.

Minimise regret, think and plan long term. A long-term plan that you keep redoing every half a year as you learn new things is better than drifting through life. Ah, and almost as a flipside of course: Don't fall for the cheap and quick happiness that gets peddled to you by advertising and other lures. Enjoy life for sure, but joy and contentment don't come from shallow moments of happiness. They come from a struggle well played, from hardship well coped with, from achievements.

And in all that, be a decent person. Let me end on this note:

(4) What would a six-year-old do?

Perhaps the most fundamental change of perspective you will take away from this book is that your preferences and those of everyone else are neither fixed and immutable nor God-given or in any other way sacrosanct. The preferences of our descendants will be subject to both biological and social engineering. So, what does being a decent person then mean going forward?

The danger is obvious: Rational thought with no grounding but evolutionary survival can lead to very odd, contradictory, and self-destructive outcomes (any cursory review of philosophy and political theory will illustrate this). With pAI and our new capabilities on top, this can easily wipe humans and complex life and thinking from the Earth.

How do you counter such runaway rational thought? I am reminded of the fact that children are often invoked as the clear and unbiased arbiters of what is indeed good. Pure and untainted truth speakers. And so my proposal is the six-year-old check. If you can explain your strategy and thinking to a child of six years, it is a lot more likely to be robust and sensible than if you fail to explain it. This forecloses many great strategies for sure, but it also kicks out many more dangerously misguided ones.

If you look for how to be a decent person in the wake of changing preferences, check in with a young child that can talk sense.

Afterword: Myths, propaganda, and wishful thinking

"και τοῦτ' εἴρηται παρὰ τῷ ποιητῇ: καὶ ἐπιστρέψας ἐξ αὐτῆς καὶ λαβόμενός μου τῆς δεξιᾶς "ὦ Πολύβιε," ἔφη "καλὸν μέν, ἀλλ' οὐκ οἶδ' ὅπως ἐγὼ δέδια καὶ προορῶμαι μή ποτέ τις ἄλλος τοῦτο τὸ παράγγελμα δώσει περὶ τῆς ἡμετέρας πατρίδος: [...] ὁ δὲ Σκιπίων πόλιν ὁρῶν ... τότε ἄρδην τελευτῶσαν ἐς πανωλεθρίαν ἐσχάτην, λέγεται μὲν δακρῦσαι καὶ φανερὸς γενέσθαι κλαίων ὑπὲρ πολεμίων: "
"Turning round to me at once and grasping my hand Scipio said, 'A glorious moment, Polybius; but I have a dread foreboding that someday the same doom will be pronounced on my own city.' [...] when he looked upon the city as it was utterly perishing and in the last throes of its complete destruction, he is said to have shed tears and wept openly for his enemies."
Polybius recalling the sacking of Carthage, 2nd century BC (and about half a millennium before the next sacking of Rome)

When you care about something a lot it is sometimes difficult to take a dispassionate view, a good hard look at reality. This is unfortunately the case for many when it comes to history and politics. Let's get rid of three common misconceptions, dear reader:

(1) "History culminates in today's world."

Now, in a very literal sense the world we see around us is of course the result of all of history. In that sense history culminates in today's world. But only in this very narrow sense.

Unlike Scipio, many of us have the inescapable tendency to see history culminating in today in a broader sense too: Culminating in the sense of finishing its journey. We tend so see all meaningful events and developments of the past as leading up to today – and no farther. And of course, this also colours our choices of what we deem meaningful and important in the past.

This simplification may be forgiven if the task at hand was to understand the present day only. If the task at hand is to understand where the history may develop towards tomorrow, however, then this is a dangerous truncation of one's thinking.

It is very easy to see this fallacy in hindsight: pick a random year in history and try to tell prior history as leading up to exactly the constellation of things in that year. More often than not this will feel like a very strange exercise because we will feel compelled to stretch the narrative a bit further to the next 'momentous' year that we remember, one that provides a culminating experience, the catharsis, the conclusion of developments. These momentous years are typically major wars, revolutions – or, for the deeper thinkers, the stretches of time where adoption of pathbreaking new technologies was happening fast in certain parts of the world.

There is a second way of seeing this in hindsight, which yields a deeper insight still. Imagine taking a random adult person from the European Middle Ages and transplanting this medieval person into our modern times. They would struggle to recognise the place they inhabited in their own time. For sure they would marvel at our technological accomplishments, at the teeming masses of people everywhere, at the age distribution of these masses and how well-nourished most people are. But quite possibly, they would feel most alienated by our general thinking and attitudes. By our individualist outlook on life, by our focus on self-fulfilment and self-indulgence, by the absence of God in our talking, and by the strange mix of homages to egalitarianism and idolatry of the wealthy and successful.

That is because the view of medieval Europeans on how the world works and should work was rooted in the Christian and in the feudal belief system. The roles of individuals, their fears and hopes, and the paths to fulfilment and happiness were governed by, first, the place accorded to families and communities in the pyramidal web of personal dependencies between peasants and their local lord, and between lesser lords and their masters. Second, by the overriding importance of family ties for economic survival. And third, by the linkage of deeds and thoughts in this life with the experience of the eternal afterlife.

You can do the same thought experiment with a random person from two thousand years ago or from twenty thousand years ago. You can also review novels and films set in the distant past and produced the recent past, and ask yourself what they tell you about the times that they were produced in. And, crucially, you can do this thought experiment with yourself transplanted one thousand years into the past or one thousand years into the future.

History does not culminate in today's world. Much like the centuries of medieval Europe viewed from today are just an episode in history, today's world is but an episode when looked at from the distant future. And much like the world view of the medieval person would be strange if not incomprehensible to a palaeolithic person, the world view of the modern Western person would be strange if not incomprehensible the medieval person. And there is no reason to believe that this flow is broken.

The world view of a person one thousand years from now will be strange if not incomprehensible – to us.

(2) "Politics is about how people *should* live together."

People band together to achieve outcomes they could not achieve alone and then fight over the spoils. This is the background to all organisations, be they political, commercial or religious.

Often, the professed target outcomes are lofty and idealistic, such as bringing about a better world and justice, peace and prosperity, equity and sustainability. While there are certainly many idealistic leaders out there who earnestly believe in these goals and strive for them, there are no large-scale organisations that are made up only of saints. There's a Wickham for every Darcy.

The actual goals of organisations are more basic and prosaic. The lofty idealistic ones are either instrumental, in other words meant to bring about buy-in and loyalty of members and stakeholders, or plain propaganda and veneer to hide the true nature of an organisation. Think of all the countries with the label 'democratic republic' in their title and how many of those are or were indeed democratic.

Beware the myth of politics being about how things should be, how a better society should be. This is either the fabrication of propaganda, or the mythology of naïve social scientists. And yet, the myth runs even deeper.

The deeper issue is a misunderstanding of the process that creates social entities and organisations. Across the ages, writers and thinkers have seen this process in 'teleological' terms, have seen it as a process that has an aim, that is developing and moving forward and upwards towards a better future. Whether we start the history of political thought with Moses or Plato, Confucius or the Vedas, what we find is thoughts on how people ought to think and ought to behave and ought to work together, and so to create the ideal society. Life and history in this thinking tradition is about people trying, and often failing, to get closer to that ideal. And as a narrative twist, their trials and tribulations are often told as Manichean struggles of good versus evil.

And this is just as true for modern political thinking. In the parts of the world with a European cultural heritage, the last two centuries have been dominated by Hegelian political thinking of history progressing dialectically to higher and higher levels. From a distance, the missionary colonialism (such as of the British Empire), Marxist revolutions, and democratic liberalism based on universal human rights are all Hegelian in their quest to realise a certain anticipated Utopian vision.

If you wish for an even more modern example, Rawls's logic of a veil of ignorance is nothing but a simplistic algorithm to compute what Utopia should look like.

Alas, moving onwards and upwards towards a fixed Utopia is not how the world works. Political organisations do evolve, but they do not evolve from primitive morals towards a certain moral high ground. The process that underlies political and social phenomena and that has generated history as we know it is much simpler and more brutal: It is an evolutionary process in which the successful crowd out the unsuccessful. The only moral maxim is 'whatever works works'. This is a basic and simple insight, yet also very easy one to forget.

The organisations and polities you see today are the survivors of a multi-millennial struggle for access to resources (including to the hearts and minds of men and women). Their inner logic is not to bring about a certain Utopia, their inner logic is self-preservation.

If you have a Utopian dream, then by all means dream it and work towards making it come true. But do not let it cloud your thinking. When looking at the world as it is you need to jettison your wishes and look at human politics the same way you would look at the political setup of a society of ants.

Or, if you prefer, you need to look at human societies the way a curious alien being would be looking. Dispassionate, and unfazed by cruelty.

(3) "Organisations are man-made objects."

This myth is a bit more abstract, so let us take it step by step. People encounter many complex phenomena in their lives. And many of the ones that they notice they try to build an understanding of. In this endeavour they will be more successful at figuring out some phenomena than at others.

Intuitively, they will be more successful at understanding complex phenomena that they have themselves created or orchestrated. If you build a complex machine, a complex Lego set or an Ikea piece of furniture, then you know how it came about. You have been there to observe and drive the process that created it. Complex man-made objects are thus among the complex phenomena that we understand best. This is where our experience and our intuition easily come together.

Of course, this understanding what one has created and orchestrated is often excessively confident, sometimes bordering on the delusional, but that is a story for another book.

And complex phenomena that are not man-made objects are often made sense of imagining them as man-made objects. This is what you read in possibly all mythological explanations of where the world comes from: a deity or a set thereof create the world, much like a human craftsman would create a toy world. And if you observe young children, you will see that they seem to naturally think of animals and machines in an anthropomorphic way.

As adults, we are likewise drawn to thinking of organisations, political or other, as man-made objects. This may seem like a very natural thing to do. Political systems are after all indeed designed by humans. Where the creator can be readily identified, we often use their name as shorthand for the system of governance they devised and established: we use the term 'Draconian laws' in almost everyday language; historians call the early Roman Empire the Augustan

Principate; the Constitution of the United States is referenced as the brainchild of the Founding Fathers; and some communist systems are called Marxist-Leninist; and so on.

If you see the individuals who devise our organisational systems are protean and free creators, then this view is accurate and we should think of organisations as man-made. If, however, you see these individuals as children of their time and their choices and designs as shaped by the constraints and opportunities of the particular circumstances they were operating in, then this view is very misleading indeed.

Alas, political systems are more akin to natural objects, or phenomena, than man-made objects. And the processes leading to natural phenomena are different from the ones that lead to man-made objects. One of the very basic and yet underappreciated differences is the source of their complexity.

Man-made objects tend to be the result of complex processes with few to many parameters; and highly complex man-made objects have highly complex processes behind them. A single workshop with regular tools and access to basic materials may be able to build a bicycle. It takes a large supply chain of specialised actors to build a car. And it takes a yet different degree of process sophistication, research and design to build an aeroplane. When people are faced with highly complex man-made objects, they typically suspect that the process that has brought these about is also highly complex.

Natural phenomena, however, are better understood as being the outcomes of simple processes; to be more precise, to be the emergent features of simple processes with very many parameters.

Think about nature. All the myriads of life forms and their interdependencies are the result of many rounds of natural selection over chunks of DNA which in turn are sequences of but four 'letters' of amino acids. Natural selection is a deceptively simple process: All sets of amino acid combinations in the DNA pool of life-forms that leverage the same resources to replicate themselves are in competition with each other and the faster replicators crowd out the slower replicators. That is really it. But run this process over hundreds of millions of years with billions of such sets of amino acid combinations and you get the astonishing complexity and sophistication of nature, including the emergence of highly intelligent life forms and what we call history.

We can also look at our own thinking, which is the emergent feature of our brains. The building blocks of brains are again fairly simple and fairly well understood. We are looking at networks of neurons, which are electrically excitable cells connected to each other and thus able to propagate electric charges from one to another. Take a small worm and all you need is about 300 of these neurons to give rise to all its muscle-based behaviour. For an ant, and thereby its well organised colony of thousands of collaborating ants, you would need about 1000 times as many neurons. And multiply that again by three million and you get to a network of neurons that produces consciousness and all of human culture. The building blocks and the processes are all the same, we just scaled the number of parameters. As an aside, it should therefore not surprise us that modern artificial intelligence models are composed of simple basic algorithms that generate complex thought patterns through estimating billions of parameters through many rounds of training.

After reading the following chapters it will be clear why and how human organisations are better understood as natural phenomena.

As a shortcut, you can also check to see that the three myths just introduced can be seen as just one myth. And that is because the first two follow from the last: If you perceive political systems as engineered phenomena, then it natural to put emphasis on the objectives that the engineer was designing the system towards and it is also just natural to imagine the engineer to have drawn on everything that has gone before to make this system the best that has ever been.

www.ingramcontent.com/pod-product-compliance
Lightning Source LLC
LaVergne TN
LVHW012116170826
845678LV00014BA/2969